SHARPER EYES OF
FaITH

SHARPER EYES OF
FAITH

A WIDOWER'S JOURNEY

HARRY STEPHEN HAGER

"Be still, my soul! thy God doth undertake
To guide the future as He has the past.
Thy hope, thy confidence let nothing shake;
All now mysterious shall be bright at last.[1]*"*
—Katharina A. von Schlegel

1   Katharina A. von Schlegel, Hymns for the Living Church (Carol Stream, IL: Hope Publishing Company, 1974).

PATRICIA HELENE HAGER
(April 2, 1955–September 6, 2020)
This book is dedicated to the memory of my
wife of forty-two years, Patricia Helene Hager.

HARRY LEE HAGER
(May 8, 1906–September 12, 1978)
It is also dedicated to the memory of my father,
Harry Lee Hager, who was twice a widower
before the age of fifty.

Contents

Preface   xii

Acknowledgment   xiii

Introduction   xv

PART ONE:

Facing Backward   1

Chapter 1—Idolatry   3

Chapter 2—Contentment I   13

Chapter 3—Future Implications of His Past Kindness   25

Chapter 4—Looking Back to See the Present   33

Chapter 5—Now the Common Becomes Holy   39

Chapter 6—The Future: Some Important Considerations 43

Chapter 7—Discarded People   53

Chapter 8—A New Identification   59

Chapter 9—The Joy of Brokenness   63

PART TWO:

Facing Forward with an Accurate Rearview Mirror   75

Chapter 10—Types of Sight   79

Chapter 11—Pressing Ahead: Philippians 3   85

Chapter 12—Beholding His Glory: By Faith Now; Face to
Face Then   93

Chapter 13—Dwellings   99

Chapter 14—Contentment II   109

Chapter 15—Many Lessons Learned   117

Epilogue   125

Bibliography   129

Preface

I write this on Christmas morning, 2020. At this season of my life, it is much easier to look back than to look ahead. At the end of every calendar year, most of us are inclined to look back on the old year and review the experiences we had. I try not to use the word "unique" for any purpose other than as a description of God. But may we be permitted to use that word to describe 2020 for all of us? It was indeed unique for me. I lost my life partner of forty-two plus years. Experiencing her death has never happened to me before, and it will never happen again. So, it was unique to my experience.

Reviewing 2020 knocks the breath out of me. To be sure, there were wonderful blessings and breathtaking experiences, especially early in the year. God held us in the hollow of His blessed hand during the dark days; but taken as a whole, 2020 was both breathtaking, and it knocked the breath out of me. Except for September 6 (the day she passed into the presence of God) to September 12 (the day of her funeral), which I see even now as through a mist, events of the year stand out in sharp relief. I remember in especially vivid detail much of the last forty-five years also. Many Christmases, especially the early marriage ones. The birth of children. Finding a church where we could flourish, serve, and be served. Moments of special intimacy. Getting our first dog. Sometimes I relive those times—I remember. I remember God's goodness. I remember His mercy to me when I failed. I remember His grace toward me. And when I remember and relive some of those times, I am usually filled with gratitude to God, but sometimes I am filled with overwhelming grief. Gratitude that is not sanctified gratitude can swiftly turn into wistfulness or self-pity. Idolatry, especially an idol lost, can cause me to focus wistfully on the past instead of on the God of my faith. How do I remember, with gratitude to God for His grace in giving me a wonderful marriage to Pat, without sinking again into the despair of an idol lost?

In writing this little volume, my goal is to learn how to redirect my focus to the future and not the past. My plan is to use God's past grace to me as a springboard to dwell more on His future plan for my life.

Acknowledgments

This book would never have been written without the input of wisdom, encouragement, resources, and comfort of many. I want to thank as many as I can think of here.

My heavenly Father has been the supreme Source of comfort throughout my life but especially during this season. He has given me hope and an inheritance. He has also given me insights from His Word that have been helpful to me and that I have tried to communicate in the following pages. Any wisdom or consolation to be gleaned from this book has God and His Word as its source.

My children, Aaron Hager, Jonathan Hager, Natalie Moreno, and Ilana Dougherty, and their families walk the path of grief in the homegoing of their mother, mother-in-law, and grammy. I have been strengthened as I have witnessed their negotiating of this path as they have depended on God's resources. They have been helpful in reading portions of the book and encouraging me.

I am deeply indebted to my cousin and childhood friend, Bonnie Bridges. Bonnie rigorously read the book and, with the skill of a creative writing instructor, made copious suggestions for corrections and improvements.

I have greatly benefited from the ministry of GriefShare, a Christian ministry dedicated to those who have experienced the loss of a loved one. My GriefShare sessions helped me to know when I was on the right track with my grieving and gave me tools to further heal.

I acknowledge, with great emotion, the contribution of my home church, Grace Bible Church of San Marcos, Texas. The Elder Board of GBC, Jim Davis, Dennis Heideman, and Tommy Jenkins, as well as many other dear friends at that church have supported me in prayer, time, and tears. They mourn with my family and me. I will never forget my entire little church meeting in our backyard two weeks before Pat's passing and singing hymns to us.

Finally, though I have already acknowledged them briefly, my thanks go to my son, Jonathan Hager and his wife Katherine. They encouraged me to write this book before I ever started. As published authors themselves, they helped me get started and they have helped see the book to fruition. They cajoled and nudged me nearly every day asking, "How did writing go today?" They have believed in the value of this project at times when even I did not. I thank them for their loving needling.

Introduction

On July 20, 2016, we waited in the hospital for Pat to be rolled into surgery. The oncologist had told her that there was a fifty-fifty chance she had cancer and that if it was cancer, it could be anything from an early uterine cancer, easily treatable, to an advanced and much more serious ovarian cancer—"ovary cancer" as he called it. Pat was always the optimist; I, the worrier. But even my worry was mitigated as we were able to video chat with our daughter, who had just given birth to our fifth grandchild earlier in the day. What a joy!

The surgery, which the oncologist had told us should last about two hours if there were no complications, went to three hours, then four, then five. By the fourth hour, each minute that went by left me more anxious. "Maybe there was just a problem with the equipment," my friend who waited with me suggested. Finally, just after 9:00 p.m., my son and I were called to the conference room. The worst. Ovarian cancer. "Will this kill her?" I asked the doctor as my son, also a doctor, placed his hand on my shoulder. The oncologist hedged. He left. We cried. So began the four years, one month, and seventeen days of a journey that my children and I took with Pat.

The day after the surgery, I, Steve Hager—elder at my church, respected spiritual leader, and Bible teacher—said to my son, "I know God is sovereign. But I don't think He loves me." I was raw. But that was what I believed.

For many days, I reflected on what I had said. And in my reflection, God showed me that for our entire marriage I had been an idolator. I idolized my wife. I idolized our marriage and our family. And why not? Was there not much in the Scriptures about the importance of marriage and the importance of children, of family? Had I not read numerous Christian books on how to have a better marriage? Had I not attended the equivalent of months of workshops on how to be a better husband and father? Educated at the feet of Dobson, Eggerichs, Gothard, and Swindoll, renown Christian leaders, I was convinced that serving my wife and family, but especially my wife, was my highest calling. There was no doubt about it, I had gone too far. My accusation against the character of God the day after my wife's diagnosis was clear evidence that I had placed her on the throne that was to be reserved for God only. Not that our marriage was perfect. Sometimes it was far from perfect. But no matter how imperfect the worship, the idol is still the idol.

PART ONE

FACING

BACKWARD

Idolatry

My plans, desires, social interactions, and values really began to crystalize during my college years. While my musical tastes were still largely informed by Beethoven, Mozart, Brahms, and Mahler, I was expanding to Blood, Sweat, and Tears, The Beatles, Chicago, Don McLean, Smokey Robinson, and Jim Croce.

In 1972, Jim Croce released a song called "Time in a Bottle." [1] It is a beautiful, pensive love song that starts like this.

> *If I could save time in a bottle*
> *The first thing that I'd like to do*
> *Is to save every day*
> *'Til eternity passes away*
> *Just to spend them with you*
>
> *If I could make days last forever*
> *If words could make wishes come true*
> *I'd save every day like a treasure and then,*
> *Again, I would spend them with you.*

1   Jim Croce, produced by Terry Cashman in the album "You Don't Mess Around With Jim" (ABC Records, March, 1972), Lyrics: https://www.lyrics.com/lyric/35313890/Jim+Croce/Time+in+a+Bottle. License permission available from https://www.songfacts.com/facts/jim-croce/time-in-a-bottle, accessed February 21, 2022.

The wistful ethos of the words, carried by a plaintive minor tune, is made all the more melancholy by the fact that Jim Croce was killed in a plane crash before this was released as a single.

It is a beautiful love song. The words, the music, the circumstances mingle together to make one desire to embrace the one he loves and never let go. Yet when we consider some of the words, ". . .to save every day 'til eternity passes away just to spend them with you," is it not true that only God is worthy of such words? Would this not be an appropriate, worshipful prayer? "God, I want to save every day 'til eternity passes away just to spend them with You."

Surely even a Christian husband and wife could be forgiven just a little bit of idolatry for the sake of saying or singing such beautiful words to one another! But this sets us up for an extra hard test of faith later if that idol is not dealt with.[2]

The Beautiful, Young Harpist

After I graduated from college, I enlisted in the army and was a member of the US Army Band, "Pershing's Own," in Washington, DC. When I finished my enlistment in June 1975, I hopped in my little red Mustang II and headed for Michigan where I would teach at Blue Lake Fine Arts Camp. My good friend was also on faculty but had commitments that would not allow him to be there for several days. He told me to introduce myself to his girlfriend, the harp teacher, Pat Motovick.

I met her in Merrick Hall, the dining hall at Blue Lake on June 29, 1975. We attended orientation together, and I walked her back to her cabin as we chatted together for the first time. I immediately noticed her gentle soft voice that put me at ease.

---

2   It is interesting that Croce did not write this song for his wife but for his son when he found out his wife was pregnant.

She and my friend dated the rest of that summer and then broke up. Pat and I corresponded a few times during the next year but neither of us was on the other's radar as a potential life partner. She was, after all, five years younger than I and still in college. I was a non-Christian "wild man" who had just gotten out of the military, and. . . well, I was no prize.

The next summer, 1976, she did not teach at Blue Lake but came back for a visit, and we each noticed something special about the other and began corresponding on a more and more regular basis. By late fall, we were writing to one another each day and opening up about our feelings for one another. I had become a Christian in May 1976, and I told the Lord that, if Pat became a Christian, I would consider that to be His go-ahead to ask her to marry me.

Pat trusted Christ in early July 1977, and we were engaged a couple of weeks later. We married on June 17, 1978. All of our friends knew that we would have a very special relationship and we did. But without me ever being aware of it, idolatry raised its ugly head.

What Is Idolatry?

An idol is any person, object, idea, or occupation that takes unto itself the worship that only God deserves. Idolatry, especially an idol lost, can cause me to focus wistfully on the past instead of on the God of my faith. How do I remember, with gratitude to God for His past grace with Pat, without sinking again into the despair of an idol lost?

The first four of the Ten Commandments deal with Israel's relationship to God, and the first two deal with idolatry.3 These

---

3   I will use the term "idolatry" in its broadest sense. Technically, idolatry is the worship of physical idols or graven images. I use it to include the first commandment: "You shall have no other gods before Me" (Exod. 20:3, NKJV).

two being the first on the list must mean that they are really important to God. (He does describe Himself as a jealous God in Exodus 20:5.) This placement also suggests that the most likely sin to all humans is taking another god. Eve gave in to sin when she took Satan's bait, "You will be just like God" (Gen. 3:5, paraphrase). Her pride got her. Pride—related to unbelief—leads to idolatry. Pride says, "I know better than God Himself." Thus, I have put myself on the throne that only God deserves.

The treachery of idolatry is that its object is often something good, like a wife or like the bronze serpent that Moses lifted up in the wilderness.

In Numbers 21:4–9, we read about the children of Israel having to go around Edom rather than through Edom. They grumbled and became impatient with God and Moses at this detour. God, who had given them so many victories, most recently over the Canaanites, and had provided for them so richly in the wilderness, now sent fiery serpents to bite the Israelites. Many of them died. When the people repented, God told Moses to fashion a bronze serpent and put it on a standard. He said that if the people who had been bitten looked at the bronze serpent, they would live. Fifteen hundred years later, the Lord Jesus Christ would use that event to explain to the religious leader, Nicodemus, that the bronze serpent on a standard, and people's looking at it in faith, was a picture of Jesus Himself on the cross (John 3:14). People would live when they looked at Him in faith. But what happened to that object, that piece of metal that had been fashioned to look like a serpent? We find out in 2 Kings 18. We learn that King Hezekiah has just taken the throne and he is instituting many reforms. We learn some of the specific reforms in the following passage:

"He removed the high places and broke down the sacred pillars and cut down the Asherah. He also broke in pieces the bronze serpent that Moses had made, for until those days the

sons of Israel burned incense to it; and it was called Nehushtan"
(2 Kings 18:4).

At some point in the 800 years between the time that God
told Moses to fashion this serpent and the time Hezekiah destroyed it, the people had lost all perspective. Perhaps they
originally kept it as a memorial to God's mercy to them. I wonder if they then didn't wrongly perceive it as an object through
which God worked His power. And then, maybe, they thought
that the object itself had power. Gradually this metal thing that
they called Nehushtan (piece of brass) became an object of
worship to which they burned incense. It started as something
good but became something vile. Thus, King Hezekiah had to
take the necessary step to destroy it.

On Loan from God

Now, up to this point, the parallel between the bronze serpent
and a marriage has worked. Something good, used of God for
His glory, becomes an idol that actually supplants worship of
the only One worthy of it. But how does Hezekiah's destruction
of Nehushtan parallel with a marriage made into an idol? God
wants marriages to endure throughout our lives on this earth.
He does not want them destroyed. But the ongoing illustration
of Christ and His bride—the church—must be under the lord-
ship of Christ, a fact which means that each spouse is on loan
from God. But how must a husband and a wife keep that truth
ever before their eyes?

A hint is given to us in each of the synoptic gospels when
Jesus tells the Sadducees (those who did not believe in the resurrection of the dead) that "in the resurrection they neither
marry nor are given in marriage, but are like the angels in
heaven" (Matt. 22:30). (Also see Mark 12:25; Luke 20:35). While
each individual believer is assured of the face-to-face presence
of the Lord (2 Cor. 5:6–9; John 14:3; 1 John 3:2), the marriages

we presently have are not for heaven. They are not for eternity. Our marriages are loaners, temporary. Does that disturb you? It disturbed me. It really disturbed me after my wife got sick. One of the best ways I know of to kill idolatry in marriage, however, is to settle that issue. Stare that truth in the face. And then, by faith, believe that God has something in heaven for you that is even better than the marriage you had on earth. What is that? I don't know. But it is relationally far better than even the best of our marriages. This we must take by faith.

I am grateful for the marriage I had with Pat, and sanctified gratitude is good. It is appropriate, and even a matter of obedience, to have a heart of gratitude toward God. It is the proper response to His goodness, lovingkindness, and faithfulness (Ps. 100:4–5). But it is not foundational. Faith is foundational. Faith, by definition, looks to the future (see Hebrews 11:1). Gratitude looks to the past. It is much easier to look back at what was than to look forward to what has not been. So how then do I use that sanctified gratitude as a springboard? How do I use that which is so easy to access what is sometimes so hard, looking with eyes of faith to the future?

Lessons in Deuteronomy

Fifteen times in Deuteronomy, Moses entreats the children of Israel to remember. Deuteronomy literally means the second law or the second giving of the law. This is not a different law than what was given already in the first four books of the Bible. It is simply a restating or a summarizing of the law for a new generation. The act of remembering is crucial.

In Deuteronomy 5:15 the children of Israel are told, *"You shall **remember** that you were a slave in the land of Egypt, and the Lord your God brought you out from there with a mighty hand and an outstretched arm. Therefore the Lord your God commanded you to keep the Sabbath day."* (ESV).

They are to remember what God did for them and some aspects of His character in doing it. He is mighty and powerful. Then they are told to obey His commands (with seven of the Ten Commandments mentioned here). Further aspects of His character are emphasized. He reveals Himself (verse 24). He shows Himself to be glorious (ibid.). He shows Himself to be great (ibid.). He speaks with man (ibid.). This sounds like a God who can and will fulfill what He says He will do. So Israel can confidently, and with sharp vision, look to the future when God says, *"Walk in obedience to all that the LORD your God has commanded you, so that you may live and prosper and prolong your days in the land that you will possess"* (Deut. 5:33, NIV). From these Scriptures, they were to remember that God delivered them from slavery, from a hopeless situation. They were also to remember that His attributes and character made Him willing and able to deliver and prosper them. He demanded loyalty, and the manifestation of that loyalty was obeying His commandments. Because He revealed Himself to be mighty, powerful, glorious, great, and the God who speaks to His people, He could be trusted to do what He said He will do in the future. This assurance of God's being trustworthy was faith-building for Israel, and it should also be faith-building for me.

I may sharpen my eyes of faith by remembering what God has done for me in the past and meditating on His character regarding those blessings. If the character of God was such that He did me great good in the past, that translates to His willingness and ability to do me great good in the future.

So What?

But the truth is that right now, Christmas 2020, I'm not much interested in looking into the future. The serious spiritual danger I suspect I am in right now is that I am more interested in remembering Christmases past than Christmases ahead. The sin of self-pity, to which I am so prone, seems attractive right now. My faith in God's working in the future of my life is less interesting to me than what He did in the past. To my shame, my default attitude toward the future is a "so what" attitude. But even here, John Piper tells me this: "Past grace is continually accumulating every day. The infinite reservoir of future grace is flowing back through the present into the ever-growing pool of past grace. . . .[A]nd God means for the certainty and beauty and depth [of past grace] to strengthen our faith in future grace."4 God said through Isaiah the prophet:

> *Remember the former things long past,*
> *For I am God, and there is no other;*
> *I am God, and there is no one like Me,*
> *Declaring the end from the beginning,*
> *And from ancient times things which have*
> *not been done,*
> *Saying, 'My plan will be established,*
> *And I will accomplish all My good pleasure'*
> *(Isa. 46:9–10).*

We already observed that the first two of the Ten Commandments deal with idolatry. This is the sin to which we are most prone, and this is the sin that blasphemes a holy God. Do you realize, though, that these first two commandments are closely linked to the final commandment against coveting? Covetousness, worldly desires that leave God out, is a powerful evil. It is the opposite of contentment. *"But godliness actually is a means of great gain when accompanied by contentment"* (1 Tim. 6:6). I wish to clarify that mourning is not sin. Grieving

---

4   John Piper, The Purifying Power of Living by Faith in Future Grace (Sisters, OR: Multomah Publishers, 1995), p. 102.

the loss of a loved one and remembering sweet times with that loved one are normal and healthy responses. Tears, many tears spread over many months after a loved one dies, are indicators that we live in a fallen world and that we were made for something better to come. Yet for me there is a fine line between normal, God-honoring grieving (1 Thess. 4:13) and grieving an idol lost. The main reason I do not want to look into the future is that I have lost my idol. I am not content with God alone. I covet my marriage to Pat. So since I can't have it anymore, I look to the past too much.

TWO

Contentment I

I have never experienced a hurricane. When Hurricane Harvey hit the Texas Gulf Coast in 2017, by the time it got to Central Texas, it was a tropical storm. But I have known several people who have been in hurricanes and have experienced being in the eye of the storm. I am told that it is very strange. What had been violent wind and torrential rain becomes dead calm for a matter of minutes. Looking around, one could see clear evidence of the destruction wrought only minutes before. And soon the storm will resume, the wind coming from the opposite direction.

What if a person were able to travel along at the speed of the storm and stay in the eye for as long as the storm had hurricane force winds? Though evidence of its power to destroy would be everywhere, it would not harm the person in its eye.

Contentment is like that. Oh, what is swirling around beyond us (relationships with other Christians, day-to-day interactions with people we see "out and about," relationships with spouses, finances, etc.) is not necessarily destructive, but it has the potential to be.

Jeremiah Burroughs said this: ". . .contentment is an inward, quiet, gracious frame of spirit, that is, the whole soul, judgment, thoughts, will, affections and all are satisfied and quiet. I suppose in the very opening this, you begin to see it is a lesson that you had need to learn, and it is not a thing easily obtained, if contentment be such a thing as this is."[5]

Believing That God Desires to Dwell with His People

One of the best Scripture passages I know on the subject of contentment, as it relates to the affairs of life, is the paragraph that starts the last chapter of the letter to the Hebrews.

> *Let brotherly love continue. Do not neglect to show hospitality to strangers, for thereby some have entertained angels unawares. Remember those who are in prison, as though in prison with them, and those who are mistreated, since you also are in the body. Let marriage be held in honor among all, and let the marriage bed be undefiled, for God will judge the sexually immoral and adulterous. Keep your life free from love of money, and be content with what you have, for he has said, "I will never leave you nor forsake you." (Heb. 13:1–5, ESV)*

The way that I can stay in the eye of the storms of life, that is to be content, is to believe that God Himself will never leave me nor forsake me. I would like to examine the implications of that truth for contentment in our daily lives.

God's desire has ever been to dwell with His children. In Deuteronomy 31, we see the children of Israel have been wandering in the wilderness for forty years and are now preparing

---

5   Jeremiah Burroughs, "Sermon I," Blue Letter Bible, https://www.blueletterbible.org/Comm/burroughs_jeremiah/the-rare-jewel/sermon-one.cfm, accessed June 10, 2021.

to enter the land that God has promised them. Moses will not be allowed to go in because of his personal disobedience to God's command (Deut. 32:51–52). But he is allowed to give a final charge to the people of God before he dies and before the people go into the Land of Promise under the leadership of Moses' successor, Joshua. In that final charge, Moses says to the people, *"Be strong and courageous, do not be afraid or tremble at them, for the LORD your God is the one who goes with you. He will not fail you or forsake you"* (Deut. 31:6). And then he says to Joshua, *"[T]he LORD is the one who goes ahead of you; He will be with you. He will not fail you or forsake you. Do not fear or be dismayed"* (Deut. 31:8). Then after Moses is gone, God Himself speaks to Joshua and says, *"Just as I have been with Moses, I will be with you; I will not fail you or forsake you"* (Josh. 1:5).

The truth that God will not fail or forsake His people in their times of greatest need has been precious for millennia. And so it is with the writer of Hebrews who is encouraging, exhorting, and instilling with confidence those to whom he is writing—Jewish believers in the Lord Jesus Christ.

I believe this thought is also precious to God. He dwelt with Adam and Eve in the Garden of Eden. He dwelt with Israel in the tabernacle in the wilderness. And, when Solomon's temple was completed in Jerusalem, God in His glory dwelt there. When Jesus came, the One whom John called "the Word," John's gospel tells us that ". . .*the Word became flesh and dwelt among us, and we have seen his glory, glory as of the only Son from the Father, full of grace and truth"* (John 1:14, ESV). After Jesus ascended back to the Father, it wasn't long until God dwelt with His children again. Only this time He—the Holy Spirit—dwelt *in* His people. And so shall it ever be, until we—the church—are called to meet Jesus in the air. Jesus will rule from His throne in Jerusalem for a thousand years, and when the new heaven and earth come, the New Jerusalem, we will eternally be with Him.

Here in Hebrews 13, he begins writing about a variety of practical issues related to God being with His children and faithful to them. The writer speaks of brotherly love, hospitality, remembering brethren who are in prison or mistreated. He talks about marital purity and the love of money. And it is in this context that he says, "*. . .I will never leave you nor forsake you*" (Heb. 13:5, ESV).

Some Implications and Applications

As we are considering contentment, I think the most important little phrase in these verses is "*. . .and be content with what you have. . .*" in the middle of verse 5. So let's look at the implications of this almighty, compassionate, omniscient Father, God's never leaving us nor forsaking us and causing us to be content with what we have. But I want to go backwards in this practical list.

Contentment in Material Goods

"*Keep your life free from love of money, and be content with what you have, for he has said, 'I will never leave you nor forsake you'*" (Heb. 13:5, ESV). What if I am in dire financial straits? What if food prices, electricity prices, car repair prices, or just the general cost of living is going up and my salary is not? "*. . .be content with what you have, for he has said, 'I will never leave you nor forsake you.'*" Let your character be free from the love of money. So, do I not plan for retirement? How much is too much thinking about money? For that matter, does it present a bad example for local church leadership to appeal for money from the pulpit or in an email? What does it look like to have character that is free from the love of money? More on that later.

Contentment in Marriage or Celibacy

"Let marriage be held in honor among all, and let the marriage bed be undefiled, for God will judge the sexually immoral and adulterous" (Heb. 13:4, ESV). What about marital honor and purity? What if a wife's husband is a different man now than when she married him? Is she not getting the support in the home she thinks she needs? Maybe the devil is whispering that lie, "I didn't sign up for this." Is it a temptation for her to covet someone else's husband? Coveting is the opposite of content-ment. *"[B]e content with what you have, for he has said, 'I will never leave you nor forsake you.'"* He who created her husband, who created her, who created her marriage will never leave her nor forsake her. And what about husbands? There is not a man among us who has never had problems with his eyes going where they should not. Some have more problems than others. *"[B]e content with what you have, for he has said, 'I will never leave you nor forsake you.'"* Then there are single people. The single may say, "I don't have a wife." "I don't have a husband." *"[B]e content with what you have, for he has said, 'I will never leave you nor forsake you.'"*

In Matthew 19, the Pharisees tried to trick Jesus with a question about divorce. In answering them, Jesus defined mar-riage as the union of one man and one woman until death parts them. He also gave some very important teaching when His disciples, grasping the difficulty of His answer said, "It is bet-ter, then, for a person not to marry" (Matt. 19:10, paraphrase). Jesus' reply to them taught about three kinds of eunuchs:

1. Those who are born eunuchs.

2. Those who are made eunuchs by men.

3. Those who make themselves eunuchs for the sake of the kingdom of heaven.

For me, at this season of my life, I am asking God to give me the gift of celibacy and to give me a new life ministry that would be difficult or impossible if I had a wife. In other words, my desire is to make myself a eunuch for the sake of the kingdom of heaven. In this way, and only in this way, will I be content without Pat in my life.

A Word Study

Before we consider the command to remember those who are in prison, let's do a word study on what it means that He never leaves or forsakes. The Hebrew word in the Old Testament that is translated "fail" (as in, "I will not fail you") and the Greek word translated "leave" or "desert" in the New Testament both have the idea of letting drop, abandon, or cut loose,[6] as in the sailors cutting loose the ropes of the rudder in Acts 27. When He says He will never leave us, He is saying that He will hold us fast. The word for "forsake" in both Hebrew and Greek is more straightforward, meaning simply to abandon, neglect, or depart from. Isaiah uses this word in a number of passages, including chapter 54, where God says that Israel is His wife and that, *"For a brief moment I forsook you, but with great compassion I will gather you"* (Isa. 54:7). But to us under the New Covenant, He promises never to leave nor forsake us.

---

6   "Lexicon: Strong's H7503," Blue Letter Bible, https://www.blueletterbible. org/lexicon/h7503/nasb95/wlc/0-1/ and "Lexicon: Strong's G447," Blue Letter Bible, https://www.blueletterbible.org/lexicon/g447/nasb95/ mgnt/0-1/, accessed February 21, 2022.

Persecuted for Righteousness' Sake

"*Remember those who are in prison, as though in prison with them, and those who are mistreated, since you also are in the body*" (Heb. 13:3, ESV). And how are we to think of those brethren who are persecuted for righteousness' sake? I think that those who have been broken, whose lives have been reduced to the level of mere survival, have learned the secret of contentment far better than most of the rest of us. This is often true even of unbelievers. I remember a highly respected, world-renowned piano professor at West Virginia University when I was a student there. He was a Latvian Jew who had survived the Nazi concentration camps. He made the remark, "You can survive anything but a bullet in the head." To that extent he was content. He realized that every day that he didn't have a bullet in his head was a good day. But think of the believer in the Lord Jesus Christ who is persecuted for righteousness' sake. Jesus must be the very air that that brother or sister breathes. We are to remember them to encourage them, but I think also to remind us to "*be content with what you [we] have, for he has said, 'I will never leave you nor forsake you.'*" I believe that this command to remember our persecuted brethren is particularly powerful in terms of contentment because we are to remember our brethren in prison, as though in prison with them. What must that be like? A dank, hot, fetid cell for the cause of Christ. Physical and psychological torture. And I am to see myself as there with them, praying for them, bringing fresh food and water, dressing their wounds. But I am in my living room with my family around and no one to come and torture me. This is beyond contentment. This is active gratefulness, and it is thankfulness that makes me act in obedience to His commands.

Real Hospitality

"Do not neglect to show hospitality to strangers, for thereby some have entertained angels unawares" (Heb. 13:2, ESV). Hospitality! We live in such a xenophobic age! I think for me the idea of showing hospitality to strangers may be the most difficult of all! It's not that I have trouble talking to strangers. In fact, I rather enjoy talking to strangers. But when I try to talk to strangers in the grocery store, it's like everybody has a mask. They stay in their own world. I enjoy smiling and saying hello and maybe even trying to strike up a mild conversation just to pull back that emotional mask a little bit.

When I think of hospitality, I think of having you into my house. I think of the Merriam-Webster dictionary definition of "hospitable." The first definition is "given to generous and cordial reception of guests."[7] But here in Hebrews 13:2, the Greek compound word that translates hospitality is *philoxenia*, literally, the love of strangers (or foreigners).[8] I take it that this definition of hospitality to strangers does not mean that I must walk up to people in the auto shop and invite them to my house for lunch (though in certain circumstances it might!), but it necessarily means going out of my way to show kindness to those I don't know. And, yes, that may take me well out of my comfort zone—stopping to help someone change a tire or pro-verbially helping the little old lady across the street. It means being a good Samaritan.

The readers of Hebrews would have thought back to Genesis 18, which depicts Abraham as entertaining angels without knowing it. He, an old man, practiced Middle Eastern

---

7   "Hospitable," Merriam-Webster, https://www.merriam-webster.com/dictionary/hospitable, accessed February 21, 2022.

8   "Hebrews 13: New American Standard Bible 1995 (NASB95)," Blue Letter Bible, https://www.blueletterbible.org/nasb95/heb/13/2/po/t_conc_1146002, accessed February 21, 2022.

hospitality, running and hustling around in the middle of what was likely a hot day to be generous to his guests. In Genesis 18:6–7 we read, "*So Abraham hurried into the tent to Sarah, and said, 'Quickly, prepare three measures of fine flour, knead it and make bread cakes.' Abraham also ran to the herd, and took a tender and choice calf and gave it to the servant, and he hurried to prepare it.*" We must understand that the heart attitude of Abraham in showing hospitality showed that he was content and generous with what he had and that it was consistent with Abraham's faith in the Jehovah who would never leave or forsake him.

Brotherly Love

Hebrews 13:1, in the English Standard Version of the Bible, says, "*Let brotherly love continue.*" This is the introductory verse to this epilogue of the letter to the Hebrews. It can also be paraphrased, "*Let love of the brethren remain.*" The attitude at the end of chapter 12 is to be one of gratitude to God because of the stability we have in the New Covenant. In light of that stability, we are to let brotherly love continue.

What's the Big Deal about Loving Money?

I want to take one more look at verse 5 and see the warning to be free from the love of money, being content with what we have, and the promise that He will never leave us or forsake us. Why is this so important?

John Piper in his book *Faith in Future Grace* points out that the Scripture seems to imply that all sin is tied to the love of money.[9] That seems a bit of a broad brush stroke to me, but it

---

9   John Piper, Future Grace (Sisters, OR: Multnoma Publishers, 1995), pp. 225–226.

is worth considering. What is it about the love of money that produces sin? Perhaps a better way of saying it is this: The same values and heart attitudes that produce the love of money produce sin. And what might those heart attitudes be? The reliance on our own resources is certainly one. The writer might have said, "Do not rely on your own resources, but be content with what you have." If I go out to dinner with someone and have offered to pay for the meal and then realize I have left my wallet at home, I am embarrassed. I am not content to let the other person pay for my meal. But trusting that God will never leave me or forsake me lets me know that God will work through this predicament. Now I am not trying to say that my embarrassment in this hypothetical situation means that I have an unhealthy love of money; I am saying that, perhaps, my pride is wounded. I look foolish. I'm humbled. I look like I'm irresponsible or weak. The truth is that God is probably doing something in my life. I probably need to be humbled at that point.

Really, when we are walking in the Spirit, we are trusting in His resources, not our own. And in this trust, we are most Christlike. Realizing this truth brings us to the cross. This matter of relying on Christ's resources and not our own, of being content in Him because He will never leave us or forsake us, is powerfully stated at the end of 1 Peter 2:22–24 (ESV):

> He [Jesus] committed no sin, neither was deceit found in his mouth. When he was reviled, he did not revile in return; when he suffered, he did not threaten, but continued entrusting himself to him [God the Father] who judges justly. He himself [Jesus] bore our sins in his body on the tree, that we might die to sin and live to righteousness. By his wounds you have been healed.

He continued entrusting Himself to Him who judges justly. He relied on God the Father's resources and not His own. During those hours, hanging on the cross, Jesus was forsaken by the Father, so that the Father could say to you and to me, "I will never, never, never leave you nor forsake you." In this, trusting in God's promise, trusting in His resources, we can find true contentment.

As I grieve and miss Pat, I must be careful not to supplant "I will never leave you nor forsake you" with "She left me and forsook me." That God remains always present in my life is of far greater importance than my wife always being present. Pat, His child, went home on His perfect schedule. Truly believing in His promise and His supreme importance will encourage contentment.

THREE

Future Implications of His Past Kindness

Jesus did not want His disciples to seek position or power as that which would satisfy. Coveting those things would surely lead to idolatry and would ruin their witness for Christ. He taught them the truth that position or power would not satisfy with an astounding act: He washed His disciples' feet.

Knowing Is More Than Head Knowledge

An understanding of God's goodness in the past makes the believer accountable for his present and future behavior. Jesus gave a very powerful object lesson in John 13. Though the actual order of events is unclear as the Lord and His disciples ate their last Passover meal together, what is clear from Luke's gospel is that sometime around the Passover meal, a dispute arose among the disciples as to which would be the greatest. It is evidently in this context that the Lord began washing their feet. If He had washed their feet, He told them, then they ought to wash one another's feet (John 13:14). Jesus, the Master, had washed their feet. Now they knew the standard for leadership, and they knew it by the example of Jesus right then in the present time. What they were learning at that moment would forever change their understanding of how to relate to one another. John 13:17 teaches how knowledge of God's present kindness affects our future action: "*If you know these things* [present], *you are blessed if you do them*" [future]. Or, as the Easy-to-Read version says it, "*If you know these things, great blessings will be yours if you do them.*" Thus, Jesus Himself modeled the standard of Christian love and servant leadership. This example set the stage for Jesus' new command at the end of John 13: "*A new commandment I give to you, that you love one another, even as I have loved you, that you also love one another. By this all men will know that you are My disciples, if you have love for one another*" (John 13:34–35).

Making It Real

I imagine myself in the upper room with the disciples and know that this One who Peter had identified as the Son of the Living God has removed His outer garment, girded Himself with a towel and is knelt at my feet; this One who has recently raised Lazarus from the dead and then entered Jerusalem offering Himself as Israel's King. I fear that I might have been among those who had argued about being the greatest. Oh, I can feel myself blushing that I could be in the presence of the Son of the Living God who was now performing the act of a slave in washing my feet! What grace! If the Lord washed their feet, could they trust Him to bless them in the future for their obedience? Oh, yes!

We sometimes lapse into despair because of the fear of the future. We see nothing but darkness coming at us. But if we could remember how God's goodness and blessing have never failed us when we needed it most, we would trust God with our future.

Just today a dear friend reminded me of conversations Pat had with her after Pat's mother died from Alzheimer's disease.

Both Pat's mother and her mother's sister died from that disease. Pat expressed to her friends and to me that she hoped she wouldn't die in that mental state. She did not. She had mental clarity to the end. It reminded me, and I thank God for this, that Pat was in no pain for the entire four-year journey, except for when she was recovering from surgery. Granted, she was terribly uncomfortable and terribly weak toward the end, but she was in no pain. Yet I ask, "But why so relatively young and why from such a frightening disease?"

Now we come to the realm of questioning our Maker. "*The thing molded will not say to the molder, 'Why did you make me like this,' will it?*" (Rom. 9:20). The One who creates is always above that which He created. He always has more wisdom, authority, and power. And even if He answered those "why" questions, the outcome would be the same. There would be no comfort in the answer.

A Fresh Perspective

It was Pat's habit to pore over the Scriptures in depth daily. During this time that was her inner sanctum, she also read Christian literature. She loved reading and praying prayers from the book *The Valley of Vision: A Collection of Puritan Prayers & Devotions*. A prayer that became her favorite and which she hand-copied for each of her children and for me is called, "The Deeps."

LORD JESUS,
Give me a deeper repentance,
a horror of sin,
a dread of its approach;
Help me chastely to flee it,
and jealously to resolve that my heart

shall be thine alone.
Give me a deeper trust,
that I may lose myself to find myself in thee,
the ground of my rest,
the spring of my being.
Give me a deeper knowledge of thyself
as Saviour, Master, Lord, and King.
Give me deeper power in private prayer,
more sweetness in thy Word,
more steadfast grip on its truth.
Give me deeper holiness in speech, thought, action
and let me not seek moral virtue apart from thee.
Plough deep in me, great Lord,
heavenly Husbandman,
that my being may be a tilled field,
the roots of grace spreading far and wide,
until thou alone art seen in me,
thy beauty golden like summer harvest,
thy fruitfulness as autumn plenty.
I have no Master but thee,
no law but thy will,
no delight but thyself,
no wealth but that thou givest,
no good but that thou blessest,
no peace but that thou bestowest.
I am nothing but that thou makest me,
I have nothing but that I receive from thee,
I can be nothing but that grace adorns me.
Quarry me deep, dear Lord,

and then fill me to overflowing with living water.[10]

Why was it so important for Pat to get that poem into the hands of her family in her own personal, very distinctive, and very beautiful handwriting? I know why. She wanted those whom she loved most on this old earth to know what was most important to her in her life. She hated her own sin. She hated the thought of idolatry in her own life. She desired to totally surrender her life to God, having greater and sweeter communion with Him. In short, she desired nothing but Him.

An article that I read recently pointed out that sin is so inextricably woven into us, from our very conception in the womb, that the only way to remove it from the soul of the believer is for the believer's body to die. Then, and only then, is the presence of sin removed from the soul of the believer for all eternity. "[D]eath," the article says, "is the finisher of sin to the godly—for by death sin will be cast out forever."[11] God gave Pat a horror of sin and a dread of its approach. And what a supreme grace it was that in bringing about the death of her body, He made it so that she would never again, in all eternity, need to have a horror of sin and a dread of its approach. For He removed my Patty infinitely far from the very presence of sin. In this I rejoice.

I'm Here and She's Not

I am here in this house we owned together. I'm sitting on a loveseat whose fabric Pat picked out, sleeping at night in the

---

10   Arthur Bennett, ed., The Valley of Vision: A Collection of Puritan Prayers
       & Devotions, (Reprint, Edinburgh, England: Banner of Truth Trust, 2020),
       pp. 134–135.

11   Tim Challies, "For the Christian Who Is Afraid To Die," Challies,
       updated January 17, 2021, https://www.challies.com/quotes/
       for-the-christian-who-is-afraid-to-die/.

very bed where we laughed, cried, prayed, and loved. And the bed in which she took her last breath. There are reminders of her everywhere. Some would counsel me to get out of this house. To remove all the reminders possible. Perhaps there is wisdom in that. Eventually. She loved this house into which we had recently moved. She loved the idea of decorating it, redoing it, making it our own. In short, my staying here is a way of honoring her. The time may come when I leave, but not yet. I am aware that this continues to root me in the past.

Earlier today, I visited her grave. My purpose was to repair some fencing around a tree the kids, grandkids, and I planted. As is my habit, I knelt at her grave and prayed to our Father. I thanked Him for His grace to us in giving us two sinners more than forty-two years of happy marriage. I don't know if this is theologically correct or not, but here was part of my prayer today: "God, will You please tell Patty that I love her and that we have one more grandbaby now?" And then it struck me. What if God did tell her that and she began praying, face-to-face to God, for our new grandbaby? Here it is! In the present! My Patty and I might still be praying together! She in His very presence. I, by faith.

The fugacious present is the key to faith. I don't know if my dear one is praying with me when I pray. But it is a faith builder to think that she might. Should faith have "might" or "maybe" as its foundation? Of course not! We read in Hebrews 6:18–20:

> [W]e who have taken refuge would have strong encouragement to take hold of the hope set before us. This hope we have as an anchor of the soul, a hope both sure and steadfast and one which enters within the veil, where Jesus has entered as a forerunner for us, having become a high priest forever according to the order of Melchizedek.

And from Hebrews 11:1, "*Now **faith** is the assurance of things **hoped** for, the conviction of things not seen.*"

The hope set before us is reliable! It is unshakeable and incapable of failing. How does "might," as in she might be praying with me, become a faith builder without leading to presumption about God? Once again, it becomes a question of idolatry versus worshiping the Lord Jesus, my Forerunner, alone. Even in glory, Pat is worshiping, not to be worshiped. So, I let "might" be "might." I let "maybe" be "maybe." And when so much darkness surrounds, even a "maybe" is a faith builder. If I were to discover, through a careful, prayerful study of Scripture that this one who was so dear to me in life has no awareness of me or anyone else on this old earth and that she is occupied only with worship and the doings of heaven, making all that she left behind irrelevant now, it would not wreck my faith. God would provide a more sure way to provide what I need.

Choosing How You Die

The purpose of this chapter has been to show how God's grace and kindness in the past must inform how we face our future. Most people would say that if they were given a choice of how to die, they would choose to die very quickly rather than from a long, drawn-out wasting disease.

Pat slipped into the arms of Jesus after four years of surgeries, chemotherapy, and time after time of hoping for permanent remission, only to be devastated by the cancer's return. At about the same time that Pat died, and less than a mile from our home, a drunk driver in a pickup truck crossed a centerline and struck an oncoming pickup truck and several other vehicles, instantly killing the driver of the second pickup truck. So, which would you choose? Most of us would say that it would depend on the spiritual state of the driver of the pickup truck.

But would that be the only factor? What if that gentleman was a believer but he had just been drifting through life? Going to church on most Sundays but largely indistinguishable from the rest of the world?[12] Pat spent most of her adult life having a strong Christian witness. But in those last years, especially, she spent time in discipleship of other women, praying for many people, and sharing the gospel with them. Before the very eyes of others, she grew in Christlikeness.

I am not far enough through the grieving process to say that I am thankful for the entire four-year journey. But there was a certain painful purity about what God did that prompts me to choose hope in His perfect plan for my future. As hope grows, so does faith.

---

12   This is all hypothetical.

FOUR

Looking Back to See the Present

*"As God's partners, we beg you not to accept this
marvelous gift of God's kindness and then ignore
it. For God says, 'At just the right time, I heard you.
On the day of salvation, I helped you.' Indeed, the
'right time' is now. Today is the day of salvation"*
(2 Cor. 6:1–2, NLT).

It's a new generation. When we began having children, the
use of a car seat was just beginning to be codified into law.
But, diligent parents that we were, we always used car seats
for our children, sometimes buying or borrowing car seats
from friends whose children had outgrown them. Car seats in
those days were pretty simple by today's standards. I'm always
amazed at how quickly my kids now are able to get the car seats
in and out of the car. And actually strapping one of my sweet
grandbabies in securely without seriously pinching a little leg
is a skill I still struggle with.

But one thing has changed little over the years. An infant's
car seat faces backwards. This is safest for these youngest

children. But at some point, it becomes safer to turn the car seat around so the child now sees where he/she is going.[13]

Several times in 2 Corinthians, Paul looks back at his experiences of God's grace in order to look ahead confidently. It's time to turn that seat around! Look at these pivot verses—hinge verses I like to call them—in 2 Corinthians 6:1–2. I noted earlier that it is much easier for me to look back with clarity than to look clearly ahead with eyes of faith. This was, perhaps, true of the Corinthian church also. He says this at the beginning of chapter 6: "As God's partners, we beg you not to accept this marvelous gift of God's kindness and then ignore it" (2 Cor. 6:1, NLT). What marvelous gift is he talking about? He is referring specifically to verses 17–18 of the previous chapter: "This means that anyone who belongs to Christ has become a new person. The old life is gone; a new life has begun! And all of this is a gift from God, who brought us back to himself through Christ. And God has given us this task of reconciling people to him" (2 Cor. 5:17–18, NLT).

The gift on which Paul wants the Corinthians to look back is the gift of having been made a new person in Christ. "Don't ignore the gift!" Paul begs them. Now Paul will look even further back to God's promise to His covenant people Israel and will quote from Isaiah 49. . . almost. Can you see the difference?

> "At just the right time, I will respond to you.
> On the day of salvation I will help you"
> (Isa. 49:8, NLT).

> "At just the right time, I heard you.

---

13   Thanks for the illustration, though in a different context, to Ron Hutchcraft in his book, Hope When Your Heart is Breaking (Eugene, OR: Harvest House, 2021), p. 143.

On the day of salvation, I helped you"
(2 Cor. 6:2, NLT).

In Isaiah's day, God is promising what He will do in the future for Israel; He will save them. But in Paul's day, the cross was past tense. So why does Paul say to these people who are already believers, "Now is the right time; now is the day of salvation"? Paul is saying, "It's time for a new perspective. It's time to act on what God has done in your life and on who you are." I believe he is further saying, "Stop wallowing and get about God's work. The time is short."

How do I sometimes ignore the gift of God? Sometimes I ignore the gift by the consumption of my thoughts on useless trivia. Sometimes thoughts are on the past. What I had with Pat. What might have been but never was. Oh, how I can brazenly waste the time God has given me! I am, in essence, ignoring the unspeakably great gift God has given me.

Be There!

Pat and I went on a church-planting trip to Michoacán, Mexico, in 2015. A brother named Patrick was one of our team leaders. On this trip, Patrick brought with him a suitcase full of raw lumber. It turned out that he knew one of the local believers and knew that his uncle, who was a carpenter, was an unbeliever. Patrick thought that, perhaps, if he could pay this carpenter to make a small piece of furniture for him, it would lead to gospel conversations. Now is the day of salvation!

So, perhaps, in my strain to see into the foggy, foreboding future, but really desiring nothing but the clear past, I am ignoring the now. I said earlier that faith, by definition, looks to the future. But a careful reading of Hebrews 11 reveals that while faith looks to the future, it is exercised in the now.

Many years ago, in my former profession, I was preparing to give a recital on the French horn. I chose the music I was going to perform and hired a pianist who would collaborate with me. I chose a man who was in demand as a collaborative artist because, not only was he a fine musician but he also had a reputation for being very creative and somewhat quirky. I gave him the music to prepare, one piece of which was particularly difficult. It would require many hours of individual practice for each of us and hours of rehearsal together. We prepared the music and gave the recital, after which my colleague returned my music to me. I was interested to see what he had written in the piano score. At one point, where the music became very lyrical and pretty, he had written the name, "Roger Williams," by which he meant, "Play this like (the great popular pianist) Roger Williams would play it." He was remembering what the great pianist Roger Williams sounded like. There are healthy ways of looking at the past.

I also noticed that in a particularly difficult part of the music, my colleague had written two words. "Be there!" When he wrote those words, he was reminding himself to be alert, to be focused, and to fully experience the moment.

"Be there" is perhaps an excellent way for Christians to remind themselves that now is the day of salvation. It is a reminder of what Jesus said in His sermon on the mount: "'So do not worry about tomorrow; for tomorrow will care for itself. Each day has enough trouble of its own'" (Matt. 6:34). It is a reminder to stay in the present.

More Healthy, Helpful, God-Honoring Ways of Remembering

Earlier, we noted God telling the children of Israel to remember all He had done for them in protecting and providing for them. As they looked at His past goodness to them, they would be better able to exercise faith because they knew His character. We noted that there is a discriminating kind of remembrance for all of us, especially for those of us who mourn. It is not a wistful remembrance focused on ourselves. It is a God-focused remembrance. But there is a different kind of healthy remembering as well, with one hand grasping the past and the other reaching toward the future.

I recently read Abraham Lincoln's first inaugural address. It is not as popular in current culture as the second inaugural address because, in it, Lincoln speaks with some ambivalence about slavery. His goal in this first address is to hold the United States together. It is a plea not to go to war with one another. When we get to the end of the speech, Lincoln says this:

> *The mystic chords of memory, stretching from*
> *every battlefield and patriot grave to every living*
> *heart and hearthstone all over this broad land,*
> *will yet swell the chorus of the Union, when again*
> *touched, as surely they will be, by the better angels*
> *of our nature.*[14]

The phrase that interests me here is "the mystic chords of memory." As the patriarch of my family, I have a responsibility to tell my children and grandchildren, as well as nieces and nephews, our family history. We recently passed what would have been my mother's 102nd birthday. She died at the age of thirty-five. By my count, there are five of us left who still remember her with any clarity. I have a responsibility to

---

14   Abraham Lincoln, "Lincoln's First Inaugural Address," American Battlefield Trust, https://www.battlefields.org/learn/primary-sources/lincolns-first-inaugural-address, accessed February 21, 2022.

tell my family about her. Why? A knowledge of who we came from in the flesh helps unify us. As Lincoln was hoping for a shared memory that would unite the nation, remembering parents, grandparents—great Christians we have known— can unite families.

The present will become the past by the time you finish this sentence. So, when awesome things happen—like a great family vacation or a great shared meal, a funny guest in the home, or a good book read together—those things that happen in the present must be remembered and retold. Even the four gospels, inerrant and God-breathed though they are, were not taken as dictation at the time Jesus walked on this earth. They were remembered stories that were later written down.[15]

So, remembering in a way that honors God is always good. Remembering in a way that draws people together as families or for some greater good is also healthy.

---

15   "How did the things Jesus said and did when He was alone get recorded in the Gospels?" Got Questions, https://www.gotquestions.org/Jesus-alone.html, accessed July 25, 2021.

FIVE

Now the Common Becomes Holy

"'Do not remember the past events; pay no attention to things of old. Look, I am about to do something new; even now it is coming. Do you not see it? Indeed, I will make a way in the wilderness, rivers in the desert'"
(Isa. 43:18–19, CSB).

At the time Isaiah penned those words, God had already brought judgment on the Northern Kingdom of Israel. The Assyrians had taken Israel into captivity from which they would never return. Now through the prophet Isaiah, the Southern Kingdom of Judah is told that she, too, will be carried away, this time to Babylon (Isa. 39:5–7). Most of the rest of the prophecy of Isaiah offers a mixture of comfort and rebuke to Judah. The end result is that God will be merciful to Judah. His covenant that He has made with the nation, in spite of their idolatry and hypocrisy, will be fulfilled.

Consider the immediacy of some of these words: "Look, I am about to do something new. Now it begins to happen!" If I were listening to the words of Isaiah in 700 BC, I would expect the New Covenant to come, not only during my lifetime, but today! I think that is what God intended. I am to live with the excited expectancy that the church of the Lord Jesus Christ might be raptured today and forever be with Him (1 Thess. 4:13–18). For most of us mourners, such living is a significant challenge. The mundane seems to remain always and forever mundane.

"Where are your raisins?"

I hate making lists because I always lose my lists. The routine that Pat and I had for grocery shopping was that she would make the list and, when we got to the grocery store, we would split the list. In the months since she left, I have gone to the grocery store when I needed a few things and would trust my memory. But last week I actually made a list before going shopping. It was a good list and kept me busy for quite a while at this grocery store with which I was unfamiliar. As I was going through the frozen food section, I noticed a sign I had never seen before: "Meals for singles." That would be me. And right there in the middle of the grocery store, I teared up. As I continued in my shopping, my melancholy grew. Then I thought of 2 Corinthians 6:2 (ESV), "Behold, now is the favorable time; behold, now is the day of salvation." So, in my thus far unsuccessful search for raisins, I began praying, "Lord, how can I break back into the 'now' and escape this melancholy?" The answer that came to me was surprisingly simple: Talk to somebody. So, I flagged down a worker at the grocery store.

"Excuse me. Where are your raisins?"

"Right back there. Aisle 11."

"OK. Thanks!"

It was a thirteen-word exchange between me and someone I had never seen before. But it tripped the switch. *Who was that guy? I wonder if he is a college student. I should go back and talk to him. No, he's busy. OK! There are the raisins.* I was released from my odious self-pity by simply saying a few innocuous words to another person and thinking about him instead of myself.

Staying in the present when the darkness comes is not the answer to the question that precipitated the writing of this book. That question was, "How do I turn my gaze from so clearly seeing the past to looking ahead to the future with a strong clarity and faith in God's plan?" But staying in the present, I am convinced as an ambassador of Jesus Christ, honors Him and protects me from melancholy and self-pity.

Lessons from a French Prison

What about staying in the present when the circumstances of the present are dark? Church history gives us the story of Marie Durand (1711–1776) the French Huguenot believer. At age nineteen, only a few months after her marriage, she was incarcerated for thirty-eight years for her biblical faith in Jesus Christ alone. Each day, one of her captors would come in and demand that she recant, and each day she would not. Every day for thirty-eight years, all she had to do was deny Christ. She didn't have to mean it. All she had to do to win her freedom, as the flower of her youth faded, was utter those three little words, "*Je me rétracte.*" I recant. Instead, with her knitting needle, she etched into her prison wall one word. "*Régistez.*" Resist. How did this believer pass her days in such dark circumstances? Her letters indicate to us that each evening she gathered the other women to encourage them in their faith. Though she herself was suffering, she poured herself into others until she was released in 1768.[16] In her dark present, she served others. "If ye know these things, happy are ye if ye do them" (John 13:17, KJV).

I have established the necessity of willfully staying in the present, serving others, and interacting with others, even on a mundane level, in order to focus like a laser on the present. In the next chapter I want to explore the future. I want to write about the present as grounding for the future and explain how to shake disinterest in the future and how to avoid fear of the future.

---

16   Francis, "All she had to do to get out of jail was to say, 'I recant,'" Huguenot Heritage, https://huguenotheritage.com/she-resisted/, accessed February 21, 2022, and John Piper, The Purifying Power of Living by Faith in Future Grace (Sisters, OR: Multomah Publishers, 1995), pp. 171–172.

The Future: Some Important Considerations

Since what started me on this writing venture in the first place was exploring how I might turn my keenness of memory into a keenness of faith in the future, I want to consider three aspects of the future: grounding for the future, fearing of the future, and trusting God with the future.

Grounding for the Future-Present Faith

In 1975 I bought and devoured a copy of Hal Lindsey's and Carole C. Carlson's *The Late Great Planet Earth*.[17] I read it in response to a summer Bible study I attended on the Gospel of John. Though the Lindsey/Carlson book had little to do directly with the gospel of John, God used that book in conjunction with the truths of John's gospel to bring me to faith in Jesus Christ. *The Late Great Planet Earth*, as the title suggests, dealt with end-time events as reported in the book of Revelation in the Bible. The book was not without its flaws. The authors

---

17   Hal Lindsey and Carole C. Carlson, The Late Great Planet Earth
      (Zondervan Academic, 1970).

speculated that events of the 1970s were specifically pointing to the rapture of the church.[18] Though this did, in one way, detract from the credibility of the book, it did communicate the imminence of the rapture.

The evangelistic Bible study in the Gospel of John helped me to understand a number of truths. The first truth it helped me understand is that God is holy and righteous, and He created all things (John 1:1–5, 29, 17:11, 25). We see here at the very opening of John's gospel that God the Father and God the Son (here called "the Word") were the creators of all that is. John uses light and darkness throughout his gospel to indicate righteousness and sin. So, God is equated with perfect righteousness in John 1:5. That perfect righteousness has shone into a dark world and was not overcome by the sinfulness of the world. Jesus Himself, in praying to His Father, addresses Him as "Holy Father" and "righteous Father" in John 17:11 and 25 (KJV). A.W. Tozer rightly said, "What comes into our minds when we think about God is the most important thing about us."[19] That perfect holiness and perfect righteousness, which is essential to who God is, has implications. As Habakkuk says when praying to this God, "*Your* eyes are too pure to approve evil, and you can not look on wickedness *with favor*" (Hab. 1:13). The sin of every single person in the world separates him or her from God. The epistle to the Romans puts it this way: "[A]ll have sinned and fall short of the glory of God" (Rom. 3:23) and "The wages of sin is death. . ." (Rom. 6:23). God told Adam in the Garden of Eden that if he ate of the tree of the knowledge of good and evil, he would die. Sure enough, when Adam and Eve

18 The rapture of the church is the event that will occur without further warnings or signs in which the church is "snatched up" to meet the Lord Jesus Christ in the air before His return to earth. See 1 Thessalonians 4:15–18 and 1 Corinthians 15:51–57.

19 A.W. Tozer, The Knowledge of the Holy (New York, NY: HarperCollins, 1961), p. 1.

disobeyed God, thereby bringing sin into the world, they died a two-fold death. Their relationship with God died immediately, and they brought physical death into the world. Tragically, the first manifestation of the spiritual death was when the humans tried to hide from God. We have been attempting to hide ever since. The first manifestation of physical death was when one of their sons murdered the other (Gen. 4:8).

The second truth my evangelistic Bible study in the Gospel of John helped me to understand was that God could be true to His holiness and righteousness and still redeem sinful people. The only way a person could be made right with God, atonement procured even temporarily, was for the blood of a perfect sacrifice to be shed in keeping with Mosaic law (see Exodus 12; Hebrews 9:22). Thus, when Jesus appeared and John the Baptist declared, "'Behold, the Lamb of God who takes away the sin of the world'" (John 1:29), he was saying that this was the last sacrifice that would ever be necessary. Jesus gave more information when He said, "As Moses lifted up the serpent in the wilderness, even so must the Son of Man be lifted up" (John 3:14). When the children of Israel were being judged for their sin, God mercifully told Moses to make a brass serpent and put it on a pole. When the people looked in faith at that brass serpent, they would be healed (see Numbers 21). Likewise, when people would, in faith, look to Jesus and His perfect sacrifice on the cross, they would be healed.

The third truth my study in the Gospel of John helped me understand was that, while God is holy and righteous, He is also loving. He loves the world, His creation. He loves the world so much that He sent His own Son, with whom He had a perfect loving relationship from all eternity. He sent Him to this old dark and evil world to suffer a two-fold death for us: death to His relationship with His Father and physical death on the cross. "'*For God so loved the world, that He gave His only begotten Son. . .'"* (John 3:16). The apostle Paul, in his letter to the Romans, put it like this: *"But God demonstrates His own love toward us, in that while we were yet sinners, Christ died for us"* (Rom. 5:8). He bore the punishment we deserved. The apostle Peter said this: *"He Himself bore our sins in His body on the cross, so that we might die to sin and live to righteousness; for by His wounds you were healed"* (1 Peter 2:24).

Fourth and finally, John's gospel tells me how to activate this love of God in my life. John 3:16 says, *"'For God so loved the world, that He gave His only begotten Son, that whoever believes in Him shall not perish, but have eternal life.'"* That is how to activate the love of God in our lives! Our response to this infinite, unspeakable gift must be belief. Not just intellectual belief but trust. You and I must trust that Christ alone could and did pay the price for your sins and mine on that cross. When that belief takes place, a divine transaction takes place. We go from being enemies of God to being children of God. We go from darkness to light, from hell to heaven eternally. Jesus Himself put it this way: *"'I tell you the truth, those who listen to my message and believe in God who sent me have eternal life. They will never be condemned for their sins, but they have already passed from death into life"* (John 5:24, NLT).

So, when I read *The Late Great Planet Earth*, when I understood my desperate need to avoid experiencing God's wrath and to be in His family forever, I bowed my knee and trusted Jesus.

In making a present decision to ensure one's eternal future in the very presence of God, ultimate assurance of a wonderful future is gained. I could go no further in this book if I did not ask you, the reader, to make sure that you, too, are assured of that wonderful future. As I said before in a different context, today—now—is the day of salvation. I urge you, if you have not trusted Jesus as your Savior, to do it today.

Fear of the Future

How presumptuous I was! I thought that when I retired, I would have a number of years for Pat and me to embark on this wonderful new phase of life. Ministry together! Sometimes going overseas together. Sometimes working together in discipleship of young couples or individuals. Sure, we had a limited number of years left, but so does everyone. Then, almost immediately, cancer happened. We did indeed have ministry together, but it looked nothing like what I had envisioned.

For one thing, it was oh so painful. How many nights we climbed into bed and cried and pled with God. For another thing, it seemed that God's people were helping us more than we were helping them. God used us, for sure. But we were so often so raw. We found God trustworthy in the pain. George Matheson, in time of crisis in his own life, said it much better than I can.

> *Oh Joy that seekest me through pain,*
> *I cannot close my heart to Thee;*
> *I trace the rainbow through the rain,*
> *And feel the promise is not vain*
> *That morn shall tearless be.*[20]

The promise of God is not vain. "That morn [morning] shall tearless be." Matheson is alluding to God's promises like that of Psalm 30:5: *"For His anger is but for a moment, His favor is for a lifetime; weeping may last for the night, but a shout of joy comes in the morning."* God also promises in Isaiah 25:8 that "He will swallow up death for all time, And the

---

20 George Matheson, Hymns for the Living Church (Carol Stream, IL: Hope Publishing Company, 1974).

Lord GOD will wipe tears away from all faces, and He will remove the reproach of His people from all the earth."

In the New Testament, we see Jesus' promise of John 14:1–3:

> 'Do not let your heart be troubled; believe in God,
> believe also in Me. In My Father's house are many
> dwelling places; if it were not so, I would have
> told you; for I go to prepare a place for you. If I go
> and prepare a place for you, I will come again and
> receive you to Myself, that where I am, there you
> may be also.'

This is an actual promise of Jesus. What is not to believe about this? Indeed, the promise is not vain that morn shall tearless be. "For momentary, light affliction is producing for us an eternal weight of glory far beyond all comparison" (2 Cor. 4:17). Finally, there is that great Magna Carta of Christian truth: Romans 8.

> For the law of the Spirit of life in Christ Jesus
> has set you free from the law of sin and of
> death. . . .But if the Spirit of Him who raised Jesus
> from the dead dwells in you, He who raised Christ
> Jesus from the dead will also give life to your
> mortal bodies through His Spirit who dwells in
> you. . . .The Spirit Himself testifies with our spirit
> that we are children of God, and if children, heirs
> also, heirs of God and fellow heirs with Christ, if
> indeed we suffer with Him so that we may also
> be glorified with Him. For I consider that the suf-
> ferings of this present time are not worthy to be
> compared with the glory that is to be revealed to

> us. For the anxious longing of the creation waits
> eagerly for the revealing of the sons of God. For
> the creation was subjected to futility, not willingly,
> but because of Him who subjected it, in hope that
> the creation itself also will be set free from its
> slavery to corruption into the freedom of the glory
> of the children of God. . . .And we know that God
> causes all things to work together for good to those
> who love God, to those who are called according
> to His purpose. (Rom. 8:2, 11, 16-21, 28)

Honestly, the rest of this glorious eighth chapter of Romans on the promises of God buttresses Matheson's hymn. If one of the promises is vain, they are all vain. Let us not get casual about the promises of God.

I have never been one to mourn angrily, but I know some who do. In the darkest times of this first year without her, in the back of my mind sometimes was this thought: *God, I'm never going to make a plan again because if it means going through what I have just gone through, forget it.* Such angry sounding words were not born of anger but of fear that, if I were to start dreaming big dreams again, God would give me cancer, or worse yet, give cancer to one of my kids or grandkids.

Trusting God with the Future

The fear that I have in making future plans has to do with an inadequate view of God. The trials and sufferings that Pat and I went through for more than four years were for the purpose of His glory in our lives and in the lives of others.

> *Every joy or trial*
> *Falleth from above,*
> *Traced upon our dial*
> *By the Sun of Love;*
> *We may trust Him fully,*
> *All for us to do;*
> *They who trust Him wholly*
> *Find Him wholly true.*[21]
> *—Frances Havergall*

What are some other subtle ways we do not trust God with the future? Have you ever been wronged and carried a grudge? Have you ever thought, *That person really needs to be punished for the wrong he did to me and God just isn't following through?*

Romans 12:17–19 (NIV) says, "*Do not repay anyone evil for evil. Be careful to do what is right in the eyes of everyone. If it is possible, as far as it depends on you, live at peace with everyone. Do not take revenge, my dear friends, but leave room for God's wrath, for it is written: 'It is mine to avenge; I will repay,' says the Lord.*"

Trusting God's positive promises like, "I will never leave you nor forsake you" (Heb. 13:5, ESV) should also mean trusting His promise to avenge evil. If God is concerned with His own glory, and He is (Isa. 42:8, 48:11), if He is concerned with His own name (Exod. 20:7), and He is, He will certainly avenge evil. But He will do it on His timetable and not before.

The implication of these truths is that when I am wronged by my enemy, I need to turn that situation over to God and let God exercise His wrath in His time. Also, I need to perform acts of kindness toward my enemy.

---

21   Frances Havergall, Hymns for the Living Church (Carol Stream, IL: Hope Publishing Company, 1974).

The wrath of God is not like the wrath of man. It is holy and, in a sense, even compassionate. For example, examine God's judgment on Moab in Isaiah 16. In Isaiah 16:11, the prophet laments the judgment that will fall on Moab by saying, "Therefore my heart intones like a harp for Moab and my inward feelings for Kir-hareseth." The lament of somber harp music is reflective of the heart of God, even in the midst of His judgment. God will judge completely and with perfect righteousness. And with perfect timing.

This lack of trusting God with the future is most often manifested in worry. But in the current era of Western culture, this worry, even among God's people, is most vociferously heard in political rantings. We tend to superimpose the latest political intrigue on the machinations of Israel's Old Testament enemies. If the wrong candidate wins an election, even many believers begin hand-wringing and worrying. My enemies must be God's enemies. We even pray cleverly disguised imprecatory prayers against those to whom honor is actually due. We do not trust that God will make all things right in His time. We worry about the kind of nation our children and grandchildren will live in, when we should be about the business of teaching them to be obedient to God's Word, to walk in the Spirit. To love God with all their hearts, their souls, their strength, and their minds. To love their neighbors as themselves.

The best way I can trust God with the future is to be about the business of ministry, doing His work. That may be writing a note of encouragement to someone who needs it. It may be preparing lessons for my grandkids. It may be sharing the gospel with someone. It may be to teach pastors in Africa.

The apostle Paul told the Ephesian elders, "*But I do not consider my life of any account as dear to myself, so that I may finish my course and the ministry which I received from the*

Lord Jesus, to testify solemnly of the gospel of the grace of God" (Acts 20:24).

My experience is that the deeper I get into ministry, the more I see God work, the more I depend on Him. I rely on Him with David who said, "I sought the LORD, and He answered me, and delivered me from all my fears" (Ps. 34:4).

SEVEN

Discarded People

There are many kinds of discarded people in the Scriptures. Lepers were discarded. Prostitutes were discarded. Eunuchs were discarded. When a spouse dies, even though the remaining spouse is sometimes surrounded and supported by loving friends and family, he/she often has a feeling that friends and family don't quite understand. Most people do not wish to reject the remaining spouse. In fact, they want to do just the opposite, especially if they, too, in the death of the spouse, lost a friend, a parent, or a brother or sister. They want to embrace that remaining spouse. Sometimes, however, the simplest situations say, "You don't belong." I recently attended a Sunday school class in a church I was visiting. I was greeted warmly and asked to introduce myself. I felt welcomed. The teacher was well prepared, and the discussion stimulated my thinking. But I suddenly noticed that I was the only single in the class. Shortly after I noticed that I was the only single, the wife in the couple next to me put her hand on the leg of her husband. *Pat used to do that*, I thought. Suddenly I was distracted, and I felt like I didn't belong. It is important to understand that situations do not discard or embrace. Situations are just inanimate life events.

While lepers, prostitutes, and eunuchs were intentionally discarded or rejected in the Scriptures, it is rare that someone who is mourning is intentionally discarded. In Christian ministry, when a spouse dies, the nature of the ministry, of necessity, changes. And I am learning that this can feel like rejection. My wife had a sweet email relationship with a young refugee girl from halfway around the world. A few weeks after Pat's death, I wondered out loud if I could perhaps write to this girl. My Christian missionary friend who heard my question said, "You probably shouldn't." Given the situation, he was right. But I felt discarded in that moment.

It is not that I am put on the shelf in terms of future ministry. It is that the nature of ministry, going forward, will be different than what I had thought it would be. I need to learn a new flexibility. And I need to learn to see ministry through the eyes of those who desire to minister to me. I can learn from them.

Lepers were discarded in Israel, not only because leprosy was such a loathsome disease, but because it was a picture of what sin is like to a perfectly holy God. But I love Psalm 103. Especially the opening.

> *Bless the Lord, O my soul, and all that is within me, bless His holy name. Bless the Lord, O my soul, and forget none of His benefits; who pardons all your iniquities, who heals all your diseases; who redeems your life from the pit, who crowns you with lovingkindness and compassion; who satisfies your years with good things, so that your youth is renewed like the eagle.*
> *(Ps. 103:1–5).*

When I think of the stigma of leprosy in the Scriptures and all the benefits of God laid out in these opening verses of Psalm 103, I am impressed that God loves the discarded. Leprosy was a picture of sin. Through Jesus Christ, God pardons all our iniquities. Leprosy was a loathsome disease. Jesus healed lepers. And while we still have cancer and heart disease and all manner of neurological disease, those too are ultimately cured in Christ. The blood of Christ broke sin and bought back—redeemed—the sinner. Jesus was moved with compassion to heal (see Mark 1:40–42). God does not promise anyone long life, but He satisfies and renews the one who trusts in Him.

Prostitution was as ugly in Bible times as it is today. The Bible does not wink at sin. *"For a prostitute is a deep pit; an adulteress is a narrow well. She lies in wait like a robber and increases the traitors among mankind"* (Prov. 23:27–28, ESV).

Yet one of the most beautiful events recorded in all the gospels concerns Jesus' encounter with one of these discarded women in Luke 7:36–50. When a Pharisee asked Jesus to dine with him, Luke tells us that a woman of the city came. And just so there is no mistake, Luke further describes her as a sinner, or an immoral woman. How had she been prepared for this moment? We are not told. It must be assumed, however, that she was a broken woman before she came into the house, because it would have required great boldness for her to openly enter the home of a religious leader. She evidently cared nothing for how things looked at that moment and even less when she stood behind Jesus at His feet, weeping. Further breaking cultural norms, her hair was down and flowing. The Lord Himself seems to emphasize the depth of her sinful past in telling the parable of the two debtors. He implies that the woman is like the debtor who owed more and was thus forgiven more. When Jesus commended the depth of her brokenness, He does what only He can. He forgives her sins, tells her that her faith has saved her, and tells her to go in peace. She now has peace with God through the Lord Jesus Christ, He whose feet she has washed with her tears, dried with her hair, and anointed with precious oil.

Eunuchs were also outcasts from Jewish society (see Leviticus 21:20–21; Deuteronomy 23:1). Yet even in the Old Testament we have indications of God's grace toward those who had been discarded when they responded in faith leading to obedience (see Isaiah 56:3–4). In Matthew 19, the Lord Jesus, in responding to the Pharisees' question on divorce, first gives them a clear answer from the letter and spirit of Mosaic law while defining biblical marriage as being between one man and one woman for life. When the disciples said, "If the relationship of the man with his wife is like this, it is better not to marry" (Matt. 19:10, paraphrase), the Lord responded by saying that some eunuchs had made themselves eunuchs for the sake of the kingdom of heaven (verse 12). He was not saying that some believers should literally emasculate themselves. He was saying that some are given the gift of celibacy to do God's work.

Far from feeling discarded or rejected, even if some tactlessly indicate this to me, I must readjust my thinking to understand that I can have ministries now that I could not have if I were married. Will I ever remarry? I don't know. That is certainly not my goal in life. My goal in life is to be contented with whatever God has for me. But for now, I will ask God for the grace to accept singleness for the rest of my life, if that is what He has for me. Jesus is enough!

Here, then, are some things to avoid saying to the one who feels discarded because of a spouse's death. I don't know anyone who would say they had never said anything they wished they could take back. I cringe at the number of times I wish I could take certain words back. Sometimes it has been that what I said was not wrong; it was just stated in an unsensitive way. Given what I am learning in this new phase of my life, here are some things I would state differently now.

1. "In some ways, a divorce is harder than the loss
   of a spouse." *That one, though not something I
   said often, is now totally expunged from my list
   of truisms. Even for the person who has gone
   through both of these, everyone's experience will
   be different.*

2. "I know you're lonely, but Jesus is sufficient for
   all your needs." *There is no doubt that this is true
   (Matt. 11:28–30). But I have found that even the
   Christ follower who is walking closely with the
   Lord can experience times of deep loneliness. God
   made us for relationship, both with Him and with
   other people. The intense loneliness that often
   occurs when one loses a spouse, or when one desires a spouse and one doesn't come, sometimes
   requires more than a true scriptural statement. It
   requires coming alongside, spending time with
   the person, and praying for the person.*

3. "I'm praying for you." *Am I really? I mean, really?
   It is better if I say, "Let me pray for you right now."*

4. "The way the world is now, aren't you glad she's
   there with the Lord instead of here?" *Again,
   there is no doubt that Pat is better off there than
   she ever was here. She is in the presence of the
   Lord and free from sin. But the surviving spouse
   needs to be pretty far down the healing path
   before he can honestly say, "Yes, I'm glad."*

5. "I know just how you feel!" *Most likely if you say
   that, you don't know how I feel. The day after
   Pat's passing, a relative of mine, twice a widow,
   sat down and wrote a sympathy note to me. In
   it, she said, "How I wish there were words to
   assuage that grief; there are none."*

These are things not to say. What, then, do you say? Often, a
simple "I'm so sorry" followed by silence is enough. But also,
we who mourn like to talk about our departed loved one. Really,

in the early stages, she is all we think about. So asking tactful questions about her can be helpful. Yes, the tears flow freely at these times, but those who listen need to be okay with that.

EIGHT

A New Identification

Back in chapter 6, I related how I became a new creation, a child of God. It was through the miracle of the gospel. But when I became that new creation in Christ, I got a new identification. Simply put, identification means that the believer's identity is in the Lord Jesus Christ. When I trusted in Jesus' finished work on the cross for my sins, I was justified before God. God identified me with Jesus Himself. In Romans 6:5 we read, "*For if we have become united with Him in the likeness of His death, certainly we shall also be in the likeness of His resurrection.*" And in Colossians 3:1–4 (ESV), we read the following:

> *If then you have been raised with Christ, seek the things that are above, where Christ is, seated at the right hand of God. Set your minds on things that are above, not on things that are on earth. For you have died, and your life is hidden with Christ in God. When Christ who is your life appears, then you also will appear with him in glory.*

Miles Stanford says, "[I]dentification is not experiential, but is a matter of placing our faith in the facts of the Word. Whereas justification has to do with birth, identification has to do with growth, which is to continue until we see Him face to face."[22]

For many years I have known that my identification with Christ was huge. If I were to grow in my Christian life, I would have to appropriate this identity into my daily life. I mistakenly, and somewhat pridefully, thought that this was my sole identity in life.

Oh, sure, it is my most important identity. However, I also identified as a musician, a teacher, a father of Aaron, Jon, Natalie, and Ilana. I took special joy in identifying as Pat's husband. How I loved being in the grocery store and having some stranger come up to me and say, "Oh, you're the harpist's husband, aren't you?" My identity as a musician and teacher ended when I retired. That was not difficult. And though I am still the father of my four children, the nature of that identity has changed as they have grown up. But it is the change of identity from "husband of Pat" to widower that has been the most difficult to navigate.

When it slowly began to dawn on me that I might become a widower, I began searching the Scriptures for didactic passages specific to men whose wives had died. There were none. Abraham's behavior after Sarah's death was exemplary in the responsibility he took for acquiring a burial spot for Sarah, for mourning her, and for continuing his patriarchal responsibilities concerning finding a wife for Isaac (Gen. 23–24). Abraham's example is a good one to emulate. But it is hard to identify with Abraham. He was married to his half-sister. He had concubines. Except for Genesis 23, we know nothing of how Sarah's death impacted Abraham and how it impacted his relationship with God.

---

22   Miles J. Stanford, The Complete Green Letters (Grand Rapids, MI: Zondervan, 1975, 1976, 1977, 1983), p. 106.

Perhaps the strangest widower story in the Scriptures concerns the death of Ezekiel's wife in Ezekiel 24. Her death and God's command to Ezekiel not to mourn was for a sign to Israel. Here again, nothing apropos to my situation.

It is in the beautiful story of Ruth and Boaz and the catalyst to this story, the broken widow Naomi, that I find the most helpful information. The story is from a time of the judges of Israel, a time when "[e]veryone did what was right in his own eyes" (Judges 21:25, ESV). And in that spirit, Elimelech, in time of famine in Israel, took his wife Naomi and their two sons from Bethlehem, which means "House of Bread," to a foreign land. In that foreign land, tragedy struck. First Elimelech died. Then, over a period of ten years, Naomi's two sons married Moabite women and both boys died without having any children. It was a story of a difficult life for Naomi as she headed back to Bethlehem with her daughter-in-law, Ruth (Ruth 1).

I like Naomi. She is not the hero of the story, but she is crucial to the story. She is flawed but faithful. For example, rather than urging her pagan daughters-in-law to come back to the land and worship the true God with her, she encouraged them to stay in their pagan land. Was she covering her own sin of being an accomplice along with Elimelech to allowing their sons to break covenant by marrying outside the covenant?

Broken and Bitter

But my main point is that Naomi was broken and bitter at the loss of her husband and sons. She reveals this condition when she says:

> 'Return, my daughters! Go, for I am too old to have
> a husband. If I said I have hope, if I should even
> have a husband tonight and also bear sons, would

you therefore wait until they were grown? Would
you therefore refrain from marrying? No, my
daughters; for it is harder for me than for you, for
the hand of the LORD has gone forth against me'
(Ruth 1:12–13).

When she returned to Bethlehem and her friends saw her, Naomi said, "'*Do not call me Naomi; call me Mara, for the Almighty has dealt very bitterly with me. I went out full, but the LORD has brought me back empty. Why do you call me Naomi, since the LORD has witnessed against me and the Almighty has afflicted me?*'" (Ruth 1:20–21). Naomi was having an identity crisis. She was no longer the wife of Elimelech, the mother of Mahlon and Chilion. She was a widow. And worse, a widow with no sons to support her. The gracious and merciful God of Israel, however, had a job for Naomi to do. And it was a job that only Naomi could perform. She was to become the matchmaker for Boaz and Ruth. And having successfully performed that great work, the women of the town considered that Obed, born to Boaz and Ruth, was Naomi's son (Ruth 4:17).

Other than those earliest days of Pat's diagnosis, I have not had bitterness toward God or toward doctors. Now that Pat's cancer journey is over, my wistful backward look toward my marriage to Pat could begin lingering on what might have been if the oncologist had done this instead of that. My identity would still have been "husband of Pat."

But even if I did not get bitter, I was and am definitely broken.

NINE

The Joy of Brokenness

"To be a follower of the Crucified means, sooner or later, a personal encounter with the cross. And the cross always entails loss. The great symbol of Christianity means sacrifice and no one who calls himself a Christian can evade this stark fact."[23]
–Elisabeth Elliot

The personal encounter with the cross, of which Elisabeth Elliot speaks, always entails loss. When a missionary goes on the field, he/she knows that loss may come. But sometimes that encounter with the cross and the resulting loss, or brokenness, is not something that is seen coming. The loss or brokenness comes without warning. In 2018, I had the opportunity to travel to a refugee camp in Uganda. While I was there, I had one of the most astounding, heartbreaking encounters I have ever had with another human being. Her name was Joy. I tell her story now to show that profound brokenness and the proper Christian response to it transcends culture, ethnicity, race, and language.

---

23 Elisabeth Elliot, "Elisabeth Elliot Quotes," goodreads, https://www.goodreads.com/quotes/255854-to-be-a-follower-of-the-crucified-means-sooner-or, accessed February 21, 2022.

Joy and I held hands as we walked along the dusty dirt road. She had been walking beside me when she simply took hold of my hand. Though I was a little uncomfortable, it is the custom of her culture that good friends hold hands (whether of the same sex or not), so I felt privileged. Joy, as a follower of Jesus Christ, is more a sister to me than even a biological sister would be—this woman, more than three decades my junior, of beautiful, smooth, black skin and for whom English was a third language.

Joy, caught in the crossfire of the civil war in South Sudan, had encountered personal calamity that is far beyond what most of us could even imagine. She witnessed her husband, brother-in-law, and eight-year-old daughter shot and killed. She herself survived being shot but the baby she was carrying did not. Like Jonah in the belly of that great fish, in a place where she could see nothing but death, life burst forth for Joy as a man preached the gospel to her. "I've lost everything, but I have Jesus now," she said to me. It brought to mind a Psalm I was reading this morning.

> *What joy for those you choose to bring near,*
> *those who live in your holy courts.*
> *What festivities await us*
> *inside your holy Temple.*
> *You faithfully answer our prayers with*
> *awesome deeds,*
> *O God our savior.*
> *You are the hope of everyone on earth,*
> *even those who sail on distant seas*
> *(Ps. 65:4–5, NLT).*

Joy was broken, but she found Jesus Christ sufficient for her every need. When I met her, her desire was to tell the other refugees that, in Jesus, new life is found. Joy would not have chosen the journey, the brokenness that God had for her. Likewise, I would not have chosen my brokenness. I must admit, however, that it seems that my life is more fruitful now than it was before I was broken.

The ultimate brokenness is death. Some believers in Jesus Christ are actually more fruitful in the brokenness of death than they ever were in life. I will tell you about one of those.

Praying with the Mind of Christ

I was present at a large conference in June 1997 when a powerful preacher from Houston, Texas, Mickey Bonner, was speaking to nearly 10,000 people on the subject of prayer. He collapsed to the ground in the middle of his sermon and died. These were his last words: "Praying with the mind of Christ comes only when we have humbled ourselves before Him; it comes only when we are broken." Brother Bonner's last words were his most important message. He named one of the joys of brokenness: praying with the mind of Christ.

Praying with the mind of Christ means praying, "Thy kingdom come, Thy will be done in earth, as *it is* in heaven" (Matt. 6:10, KJV). Yet how often have we prayed that with rote insincerity? How often? What if each time we prayed that prayer we really meant, "God, do *Your* will here. In this world. In my life. Do it as perfectly as You do it in heaven"? His will. No matter what. What are the implications of that? If I think of all the things that could mean, it would be staggering. But to pray like Jesus taught us, with His mind, requires brokenness.

It sticks in my throat to say that Joy was privileged to be broken in witnessing the deaths of her family. It sticks in my throat to say that Pat passing away and leaving me a widower was a rare blessing. Yet must Joy and I and all followers of the Crucified rejoice in our brokenness? Embrace our brokenness?

Both Elisabeth Elliot and Mickey Bonner seem to say, "Yes, embrace it." And it may be that our profound brokenness will bring glory to God.

There are those believers whom God calls to this sacred ministry of brokenness to comfort others who are suffering. Tim Challies says this:

> *Those he calls are ordained to it not by the laying on of hands but by the emptying of their arms, the breaking of their bodies, the shattering of their hearts. He calls them to lose so they might bless, to grieve so they might comfort, to suffer so they might strengthen, to endure so they might encourage. He calls them to submit to him in their sorrows, that they might be a light in the darkness, a song in the night.*[24]

Brokenness Is More Than I Thought

Brokenness means to have one's heart broken, which is to say that the site of his affections experiences devastation. A broken heart always involves loss: the loss of the life of a loved one, the loss of a dream, the loss of health, the loss of a marriage or other relationship. But brokenness is more than having a broken heart. It means a paradigm shift in major areas of one's life. In my case, the day Pat died I said, "I don't know how to be." And I still don't.

In some ways, it's like experiencing adolescence all over again. How does a widower act? How do I interact with women without them thinking I'm being aloof or too familiar? How do

---

24   Tim Challies, "The Ministry of Sorrow," Challies, updated May 17, 2021, https://www.challies.com/articles/the-ministry-of-sorrow/.

I know when my voice sounds too strident without Pat there to put her hand on my knee? How do I respond when I am invited to someone's home and I'm just not ready? For that matter, what if I do interact with others in inappropriate ways? How will I know that? How will I fix it? Is my forgetfulness the infamous widower's fog, or is it just old age forgetfulness?

The idea of victimhood can easily creep into the thinking of the broken one. The seemingly haphazard nature of the waves of grief as well as those socially difficult times when the broken one does not know how to be can lead to self-pity. The broken one must guard against that.

Don't Waste Your Brokenness

I have imbibed deeply of John Piper's writings for the purposes of this book as well as at other times in my life. His book, *Don't Waste Your Life*,[25] was his first book that Pat and I read together, and it was life-changing. After he was diagnosed with prostate cancer, he wrote an article called "Don't Waste Your Cancer."[26] I say to myself, and to other broken people, let's not waste our brokenness.

How might we waste our brokenness? Certainly, we can waste it by becoming bitter, as I was right after Pat was diagnosed. We can waste it by withdrawing. (My brother, a pastor in West Virginia, tells of a woman whose husband died several years ago who has stopped going to church and rarely interacts with anyone.) We can also squander our brokenness by trying to escape, by trying to reason our way out of the brokenness. "I'm lonely. What shall I do? I know! I'll find the first available

---

25 John Piper, Don't Waste Your Life (Wheaton, IL: Crossway Books, 2007).

26 John Piper, Don't Waste Your Cancer (Wheaton, IL: Crossway Books, 2011), https://document.desiringgod.org/don-t-waste-your-cancer-en.pdf?ts=1439242114, accessed February 21, 2022.

woman and marry her!" I have known people who tried to escape brokenness with human reasoning. It led to deeper and more serious brokenness. Trying to medicate with drugs or alcohol. Some become workaholics. Others indulge in habitual self-pity. None of these escapes glorify God and they waste our brokenness that God wants to use.

The worst part of trying to escape brokenness, however, is that we deprive other sufferers of inhaling the sacred aroma of an alabaster vial broken and its precious contents poured on the feet of Jesus for His service. We deprive our fellow sufferers of witnessing the holy, intimate sweetness of a child of God embraced by Him, dwelling in His shadow, walking in the Spirit, and displaying fruit for His glory and the benefit of other sufferers.

The holily broken believer may pray:

Thou hast disarmed me of the means in which I trusted,
and I have no strength but in thee.
Thou alone canst hold back my evil ways,
but without thy grace to sustain me I fall.
Satan's darts quickly inflame me,
and the shield that should quench them
easily drops from my hand:
Empower me against his wiles and assaults.
Keep me sensible of my weakness,
and of my dependence upon thy strength.
Let every trial teach me more of thy peace,
more of thy love.[27]

---

27 Arthur Bennett, ed., The Valley of Vision: A Collection of Puritan Prayers & Devotions, (Reprint, Edinburgh, England: Banner of Truth Trust, 2020), p. 311.

Ways to Use My Brokenness

1. TO COMFORT OTHERS

> *"Blessed be the God and Father of our Lord*
> *Jesus Christ, the Father of mercies and God of*
> *all comfort, who comforts us in all our afflic-*
> *tion so that we will be able to comfort those who*
> *are in any affliction with the comfort with*
> *which we ourselves are comforted by God"*
> *(2 Cor. 1:3–4).*

When I meet someone who is going through a similar journey to mine, rather than being sad for myself, I feel encouraged and blessed to have the opportunity to walk with that person, even if only for a little while, on a path with which I am so familiar. I can be that person's coach if she/he will allow.

My coach is a man named Simon whose wife passed into the presence of the Lord a couple of years before Pat. When I was having a tough time a couple of months ago, I told Simon about how one of those unexpected waves had come and I had wept like a baby. He responded, "Good job!" That was exactly what I needed. It was not the comfort a widow would give to her grieving sister but it was exactly right—man-to-man.

2. AS A POWERFUL WEAPON AGAINST SIN

> *"Hide Your face from my sins and blot out all my*
> *iniquities. Create in me a clean heart, O God, and*
> *renew a steadfast spirit within me"*
> *(Ps. 51:9–10).*

The story of King David's sin with Bathsheba is well-known (see 2 Samuel 11). This man after God's own heart went from being an irresponsible king to being an adulterer to being a liar to being a murderer. Sometime after David's sin was confronted by the prophet Nathan (see 2 Samuel 12) and David confessed his sin to God and repented, he penned the words to Psalm 51. The entire psalm should be studied to really dig into this idea of brokenness leading to hatred of sin. These verses drip with contrition and brokenness.

It was sin that caused your brokenness, not that there was necessarily sin on your part or on the part of another, but it was, at a minimum, Adam's sin. It was sin—not His own but ours—that sent Jesus on His mission to the cross. This can be a powerful motivator to hate sin.

3. TO REMOVE THE FEAR OF DEATH

> *"Therefore, since Christ has suffered in the flesh, arm yourselves also with the same purpose, because he who has suffered in the flesh has ceased from sin, so as to live the rest of the time in the flesh no longer for the lusts of men, but for the will of God"* (1 Peter 4:1–2).

When this Scripture says that Christ has suffered in the flesh, it means that He died (see the previous verses at the end of chapter 3). Why should I set death as my purpose? Why should I arm myself or furnish myself with death? What an odd thing for Peter to write! Not really, for then Peter states the obvious: *"[H]e who has suffered in the flesh **[died]** has ceased from sin."* So right. Though it is in our old nature to fear death, the knowledge that I will never again need to say, "I'm sorry" to God or anyone else after I die goes a long way toward removing the fear of death.

> *"And He went a little beyond them, and fell on His*
> *face and prayed, saying, 'My Father, if it is possi-*
> *ble, let this cup pass from Me; yet not as I will, but*
> *as You will'"*
> *(Matt. 26:39).*

Three times our Lord prayed this prayer. Our precious Lord did not want to face death any more than you and I want to face death. He dreaded having His relationship with His Father broken. That relationship, which had been for all eternity, was broken during those terrible hours when He was on the cross.

The ultimate brokenness is death. Yet, in His submission to the Father, Jesus tasted death for all of us and was death's conqueror for all of us. So that when that moment of ultimate brokenness comes for each of us, it should be a reminder that our Savior was broken for all of us so that brokenness will itself be broken forever.

The Promise of God

What a comfort are the promises of God!
Those precious promises.

> *The LORD is near to the brokenhearted*
> *And saves those who are crushed in spirit*
> *(Ps. 34:18).*

Notice that we are not promised a specific ending time to our brokenness. Nor are we promised that because we are

His sons and daughters that our brokenness will be less than
that of others.

> *For his anger lasts only a moment,*
> *but his favor lasts a lifetime;*
> *weeping may stay for the night,*
> *but rejoicing comes in the morning*
> *(Ps. 30:5, NIV).*

> *And we know that God causes all things to*
> *work together for good to those who love God, to*
> *those who are called according to His purpose. For*
> *those whom He foreknew, He also predestined to*
> *become conformed to the image of His Son, so that*
> *He would be the firstborn among many brethren*
> *(Rom. 8:28–29).*

James A. Stifler says this concerning Romans 8:28–29:

> *The present verse asserts the fact that God is*
> *making all things work together for the good of*
> *His people; the next verse gives the reason for the*
> *fact in His predestinating them from the begin-*
> *ning to be like His Son. What He has determined*
> *at the beginning to accomplish, nothing along the*
> *way can thwart. His predetermination controls*
> *everything affecting those who love Him.*[28]

---

28   James A. Stifler, The Epistle to the Romans (Thirteenth printing, Chicago,
     IL: The Moody Bible Institute of Chicago, 1979), p. 146.

PART TWO

FACING
FORWARD WITH
AN ACCURATE
REARVIEW
MIRROR

Today is June 17, 2021. It would have been our forty-third anniversary. Today I have intentionally immersed myself in the past. I am wearing both of our wedding rings on a chain around my neck. Today only. I got Pat an anniversary card, wrote her a note like I nearly always did on our anniversary, planted her favorite flowers in the front of the house, and in a little while, will visit her grave and place silk flowers. Why would I start this section on facing forward by writing about how much I'm looking back today? It is because my purpose in facing forward is not to "move on" with my life. It is not to make things that used to be important to me unimportant. My purpose is to move ahead. Without a good rearview mirror, I am not able to have a healthy understanding of all the grace God has worked into my life and all the grace He will work into my life until it is time for me to fly to His presence.

I am reminded of the 2006 Pixar movie, *Cars*.[29] Lighting McQueen, the hotshot race car, existed for one purpose: to be fast. But that meant that to be streamlined, he could have no rearview mirrors. His tow truck friend, Mater, had to teach him how to look behind him and back up, and it paid dividends in the big championship race. To move forward in a spiritually healthy way, I need to occasionally look back.

We who grieve have the backward look as our default. But now, I will look ahead. And to look ahead, I need sharper eyes of faith.

---

29 Cars, directed by John Lasseter, produced by Pixar Animation Studios (Emeryville, CA: 2006).

TEN

Types of Sight

When my eldest son got his first pair of glasses at age ten, he was beside himself with delight that he could see so many things he hadn't seen in a very long time. He was thrilled. I, on the other hand, could be a very morose child. When I got my first pair of glasses at about the same age, I was beside myself with worry. *If I already need glasses at such a young age*, I thought to myself, *I'll be blind by the time I'm an adult*! It was a matter of perception, of perspective. I was not thinking about the new world or the new opportunities that were open to me because my vision had been corrected. (I was never a star baseball player, but my skills improved dramatically when my sharpened visual acuity allowed me to gauge the speed of the ball coming toward me more accurately.) But my son was right. Clear vision means that I can see new doors of opportunity open.

Let's think about the prophet Elisha for a moment. Elisha, whose prophetic ministry was from ca. 856 BC to ca. 797 BC,[30] was the successor to the mighty prophet Elijah. Elisha had been Elijah's loyal assistant and, when it was time for God to take Elijah back to heaven, Elisha somehow knew that the time

---

30   Merrill F. Unger, Unger's Bible Dictionary (Chicago, IL: Moody Press, twenty-fourth printing, 1976), pp. 307, 559.

of his master's departure was close. Three times in these final days of Elijah's ministry, he told Elisha to stay while he departed for the next town. And three times Elisha refused, first in Gilgal, then in Bethel, and finally in Jericho (2 Kings 2:1–6). After Elijah struck the waters of the Jordan River with his mantle, thereby separating the waters so he and Elisha could cross over, Elisha asked for a double portion of Elijah's spirit. Elijah told him that if he saw him going up to heaven, that meant that Elisha would have his request. Elisha did indeed see Elijah taken up to heaven. When he took Elijah's mantle that had fallen from him and struck the Jordan River, the waters again separated, and Elisha crossed back over (2 Kings 2:9–14).

We often leave the story there. But there is one more important part. There had been schools of prophets in Bethel and in Jericho. Some of the sons of the prophets in Jericho decided to wait on the west side of the Jordan to see what would happen when Elijah and Elisha crossed over. They evidently had seen the whirlwind, but they had not seen what happened to Elijah. They suggested that, perhaps, God had picked him up and put him back down on a distant mountain (2 Kings 2:16). They were not given the eyes to see the reality of the situation; God had sent a fiery chariot to take Elijah to heaven (2 Kings 2:11). It requires the eyes of special revelation to see what God is doing.

Another time, when the Arameans were plotting to capture Elisha because he always seemed to know their war plans against Israel, the king of Aram, Ben-Haddad, sent troops to capture him at Dothan. (Did it not occur to Ben-Haddad that if God had told Elisha of Ben-Haddad's plans against Israel, He might have told Elisha of Ben-Haddad's plans against him?) Scripture tells us that when Elisha's servant awoke one morning and saw the city surrounded by Arameans, he was quite alarmed. He came back to Elisha with the question many ask in times of fear or other extremity: "What shall we do?" (2 Kings 6:15). Elisha's answer must have seemed non-sensical to the servant. "'Do not fear, for those who are with us are more than those who are with them'" (verse 16). Then Elisha prayed, "'O LORD, I pray, open his eyes that he may see'" (verse 17). Then the servant was able to see the army of flaming horses and chariots all around. He was able to see that army coming to Elisha's aid and God striking blind the Aramean army. Then Elisha, in delicious irony, led them blind to the king of Israel and again prayed, "'O Lord, open the eyes of these *men*, that they may see'" (verse 20). When their eyes were opened, they saw that they were in the midst of their enemy Israel! Israel's king would have killed them, but Elisha, communicating God's mercy, told the king to feed them, give them drink, and sent them away to their master, Ben Haddad.

Elisha's servant had his eyes opened to the reality of God's protection, while the pagan army had their eyes opened to danger of their situation. Today, we as God's children need our eyes opened to the former, while the enemies of God (anyone who has never trusted Jesus as Savior) need eyes opened to their eternal danger.

I pray, "O God, open my eyes to see the blessed protection and abundance I have from You, even when all around me things appear exactly opposite." For the lost, I pray, "O God, open their eyes to the terrible danger they face even as they say 'peace and safety.'"

I love the biblical word, "behold." In our English usage there is usually the idea of seeing something. As the word is used biblically, particularly in Hebrew, it can be used to express surprise or to pay special attention to something. The Hebrew word used in the context of Elisha's story, when he prays for God to open eyes that they may see, is a different word than for the word "behold." The word in Elisha's story is הָאֵר, *rā â*, which can mean not only to physically see, but to perceive or understand. But when we see the word, "behold," it is rather like the politician who starts the answer to a question with the word, "look," or the preacher who begins to make an important point with the words, "Watch this," meaning, "Pay attention!"[31]

The New Testament passage that most captures the hope we have in Christ uses both of these ideas. To see or perceive and to pay attention. "And I saw [perceived] heaven opened, and behold [pay attention], a white horse, and He who sat on it *is* called Faithful and True, and in righteousness He judges and wages war" (Rev. 19:11).

Oh, how often I sleepwalk through life! If I could walk in the Spirit with more spiritual alertness to God's work in His world rather than having my perceptions and my attention drawn inward, I would be less inclined to look backward. I would look to the future with sharper eyes of faith. I need lenses ground from Scripture truth. Is there an army of flaming chariots around me? I don't know. I can't see. Do I have a guardian angel watching over me and protecting me at every moment? I might infer that from Psalm 91:11–13, but I can't know that this is constant.

What I do know from these Scripture-ground lenses is that I am indwelt by the Holy Spirit (John 14:16–17). And it is He who gives sight beyond even that which Elisha's servant was given. Paul prayed in Ephesians 1:17–20 (NIV):

> *I keep asking that the God of our Lord Jesus Christ,*
> *the glorious Father, may give you the Spirit*[32] *of*

---

31 "Lexicon: Strong's H7200," Blue Letter Bible, https://www.blueletterbible.org/lexicon/h7200/nasb95/wlc/0-1/, accessed August 3, 2021.

32 Most modern translations indicate that this is not a direct reference to the Holy Spirit by using "spirit of wisdom." It is still, at a minimum, an indirect reference to the Holy Spirit, since any wisdom or revelation must be endowed by the Holy Spirit. Isaiah 11 reveals seven characteristics of the Spirit of God, one of which is wisdom.

wisdom and revelation, so that you may know
him better. I pray that the eyes of your heart may
be enlightened in order that you may know the
hope to which he has called you, the riches of his
glorious inheritance in his holy people, and his in-
comparably great power for us who believe. That
power is the same as the mighty strength he exert-
ed when he raised Christ from the dead and seated
him at his right hand in the heavenly realms.

My looking ahead with sharper eyes of faith is only possible
when I am filled with the Holy Spirit. Instead of seeing Elijah
taken to heaven in a whirlwind, I am given the ability to know
the One who took Elijah to heaven better. Instead of seeing
the flaming chariots surrounding Elisha and his servant, I am
given sharp vision to see the hope of His calling, the riches of
His inheritance, and His mighty resurrection power toward
me. And, I might add, toward the one I love and miss so much
in this life.

ELEVEN

Pressing Ahead: Philippians 3

"[B]ut one thing I do: forgetting what lies be-hind and reaching forward to what lies ahead, I press on toward the goal for the prize of the up-ward call of God in Christ Jesus"
(Phil. 3:13–14).

Many who have lost a spouse cling doggedly to the memory of that spouse. I have noticed that as the months begin to add up since Pat's homegoing, certain details of our life together have already begun to fade. This bothers me. Must the healing from this amputation mean that I forget that I ever had two legs? If I can learn to travel this widower's journey reasonably well as half of myself, does that mean forgetting that I was ever whole?

Or was I whole? Well, I was as whole as any mortal dares think himself to be. I married a beautiful, bright woman who was committed to loving God and loving her family. We sub-mitted to God's leading, and she submitted to my leading. We had five wonderful children, one of whom is in heaven now because of miscarriage. We had sweet times together camping, visiting extended family in New York and West Virginia, biking, fishing, and vacationing. All of our kids married godly spouses. My work, while challenging at times, always put food on the table. We had a fulfilling love life and sublime times in God's Word and in prayer. But did those things make me whole?

The apostle Paul put it this way in Philippians 3:7–8:

> *But whatever things were gain to me, those things I have counted as loss for the sake of Christ. More than that, I count all things to be loss in view of the surpassing value of knowing Christ Jesus my Lord, for whom I have suffered the loss of all things, and count them but rubbish so that I may gain Christ.*

The rest of Philippians 3 is about this forward reach stated in verses 13–14 in this chapter heading. The desire to live godly in Christ Jesus. Philippians 3:8 encapsulates the whole purpose of this book, and verse 9 continues the thought: "*[A]nd may be found in Him, not having a righteousness of my own derived from the Law, but that which is through faith in Christ, the righteousness which comes from God on the basis of faith.*"

These verses mean that every follower of Jesus Christ is to have this forward reach. Every Christian is characterized by being found in Him, that is, identified with Him, having been justified[33] when that Christian trusted that Christ paid the penalty for his/her sin. The believer has no righteousness based on what that person has or has not done, nor does he have righteousness based on who he is, no matter what his family

---

33   Justification is a theological term which, simply put, means that a person is declared righteous. Justification is an act of God whereby He pronounces a sinner to be righteous because of that sinner's faith in Christ.

background is. A good marriage, a good family does not make one right before God. Only Jesus is enough to do that. Gaining Christ sounds like a work that the believer does. It is not. To explain what gaining Christ is, we must look a few verses later. *"Not that I have already obtained it or have already become perfect, but I press on so that I may lay hold of that for which also I was laid hold of by Christ Jesus"* (Phil. 3:12).

There is one Greek word in that last clause that is the key in what it means to gain Christ. καταλαμβάνω *Katalambano* means to lay hold of so as to make one's own.[34] Christ made me His own that I might make His upward call my own (verse 14). But notice that even the great apostle says that he is still working on it. He is using the language of one who is straining and striving, leaning into the storm so that the sunny blue skies of the consummated upward call will one day be his. This prize of the upward call is our sanctification. The day will come when our sanctification is complete. When we are forever in His presence at the rapture of the church or one second after our heart beats its last on this old earth, we will know Christlikeness to the fullest. The four yearnings of verse 10 will be fulfilled:

1. The believer will know Him.

2. The believer will know the power of His resurrection.

3. The believer will know the fellowship of His sufferings.

4. The believer will be conformed to His death.

---

34   "Lexicon: Strong's G2638 - katalambanō," Blue Letter Bible," https://www.blueletterbible.org/nasb95/phl/3/12/p0/t_conc_1106012, accessed February 21, 2022.

And, though every believer through all history up to this very moment still lacks a resurrection body, those now with the Lord see Jesus in His glorious resurrection body. Each of us will have a literal resurrection body one glorious day.

Running Hard and Hot

Twice Paul says in this passage that he presses on (verses 12 and 14). One of the meanings of the Greek word that is used here has to do with running a race and looking to the goal. I am reminded of the days when running was my hobby. Sometimes, especially in the Texas summers, I would wait until too late in the day to begin my run and the temperature would already be hot. But that was an additional challenge. So, I would often make myself run the full course, no matter how hot, how exhausted I was. I would press on until I got back home. Frequently I would stagger into the house, collapsing on the floor under the ceiling fan. Pat's response was frequently a mixture of annoyance and real concern that this time I had pushed myself too hard. But after I had cooled down, I always felt great for the rest of the day. I think that was a microcosm of what Paul was describing.

In a comprehensive sense, when Paul writes about the upward call, he is speaking of that which is consummated in our glorification, summarized in Philippians 3:20–21:

> For our citizenship is in heaven, from
> which also we eagerly wait for a Savior, the
> Lord Jesus Christ; who will transform the body of
> our humble state into conformity with the body of
> His glory, by the exertion of the power that He
> has even to subject all things to Himself.

As I was able to discipline my body to run in temperatures well over 90° "just because," should not I, as a follower of Jesus Christ, empowered by God, the Holy Spirit, be able to press on toward maturity in Jesus Christ and to walk in the Spirit and manifest that fruit?

I love what Dr. John Piper said to a young Christian woman who was despondent and wanted to die and go to heaven because of the mess she had made of her life. Piper said, "Yes, Marissa, long for heaven, long for Christ, long for the day when we will sin no more. But trust his promises now, like Paul as he faced a painful future and walked by faith, not by sight. God's promise for you is fruit in the midst of this sorrow."[35]

Run toward the Roar

Levi Lusko in his book, *Through the Eyes of a Lion*, points out that the male lion has an imposing mane and an intimidating roar (see 1 Peter 5:8). Yet it is the stealthy lioness who does most of the hunting and killing. Often it is the roar of the male that sends the prey running away and straight into the clutches of the waiting female. Then Lusko writes the following:

> *It's shocking how often that is true. When you run from things that scare you, you move toward danger, not away from it. If you fail to face your fears, they will always be right there behind you. You must suppress the little voice inside that's telling you to get out of Dodge. It is not your friend. When you feel that panicky fight or flight sensation*

35   John Piper, "Is It Sinful to Want to Die?" Desiring God, updated May 13, 2019, https://www.desiringgod.org/interviews/is-it-sinful-to-want-to-die.

> *and you want to run away, do the opposite. Run*
> *toward the roar. You have come into the kingdom*
> *for just such a time as this (Esther 4:14).*[36]

Pressing on to maturity in Christ is like that often. Doing the hard things, dying to self, that Christ might be manifest in me, is like running toward danger, not away from it. Running toward the roar and leaning into the storm are actions and attitudes we must cultivate. They are counterintuitive to our pathetically frail natures. So, when I wore our wedding bands on our anniversary and wrote a note to Pat, there was a sense in which I was running toward the roar. I was cultivating a deeper trust in Christ's provision for me.

Fearing God

Fearing God is the key to doing these hard things. Part of fearing God is indeed a reverential trust, as C.I. Scofield says.[37] Before one trusts Christ as Savior, a trembling, real fear is appropriate. This is not just an Old Testament concept. The Lord Jesus Himself said, "But I will warn you whom to fear: fear the One who, after He has killed, has authority to cast into hell; yes, I tell you, fear Him!" (Luke 12:5). A man came up to me after church one Sunday and told me that he needed to know how to be right with God because he didn't want to burn in hell. I got to tell him how to be right with God through faith in the Lord Jesus Christ, and he prayed to trust Him. That was an appropriate, trembling fear of God. But once

---

36   Levi Lusko, Through the Eyes of a Lion: Facing Impossible Pain, Finding Incredible Power (Nashville, TN: W Publishing Group/Thomas Nelson, 2015), p. 158.

37   C.I. Scofield, editor, The New Scofield Reference Bible-Authorized King James Version (New York, NY: Oxford University Press, 1967), footnote on p. 609.

a person is saved, that trembling fear disappears and a sense of awe and reverence for what God did for us through the Lord Jesus Christ takes over.

The fear of the Lord is a sliding scale. The trembling fear comes first for the judgment that God has every right to exact on sinful man. But once a person understands what God has done so that His judgment falls on Another, instead of the sinner, the sinner begins to have an awe, a reverence, and even a love for God. So when Solomon says, "The fear of the LORD is the beginning of knowledge" (Prov. 1:7), and Paul says, *"Therefore, having these promises, beloved, let us cleanse ourselves from all defilement of flesh and spirit, perfecting holiness in the fear of God"* (2 Cor. 7:1), we see that the fearing God scale has gone from shrinking back in fear, to adoration. Think about it. Jesus has power over the devil and over death itself (2 Tim. 1:10; Heb. 2:14–15). There is nothing that, in our humanity, we fear as much as death. Yet Jesus defeated the devil and death itself. Such a Person is worthy of our awe, our reverence, and, yes, our fear. But it is a fear that means, "I don't fear the storm. I don't fear the roar." And, as this becomes our practice, we come closer and closer to that day when the faith shall be sight. Not only will the backward look hold no interest for me, it will be obscured in the glory of His countenance. What is more, *"[The Lord Jesus Christ] will transform the body of our humble state into conformity with the body of His glory, by the exertion of the power that He has even to subject all things to Himself"* (Phil. 3:21).

He has the power to subject all things. Romans 8:38–39 list all those things: life, death, angels, principalities, powers, things present, things to come, powers, height, depth, all other created things. That includes the subjection of cancer, rejection, distractions, politics, persecution to Himself. Fear? What fear? Lean into the storm. Run toward the roar.

TWELVE

Beholding His Glory: By Faith Now; Face to Face Then

"But we all, with unveiled face, beholding as in a mirror the glory of the Lord, are being transformed into the same image from glory to glory, just as from the Lord, the Spirit" (2 Cor. 3:18).

And what do we get as believers in the Lord Jesus Christ when we lean into the storm, when we run toward the roar? Shining light, mirrors, transformation, glory. We get these things now by faith. We who have trusted Christ and are indwelled by the Spirit of the Lord—the Holy Spirit—have unveiled faces. This indwelling and unveiling means that we are given understanding in this New Covenant age that those of the Old Covenant did not have. Even the Old Testament heroes of faith from Hebrews 11 did not understand those of us under the New Covenant. Hebrews 11:39–40 says, "And all these, having gained approval through their faith, did not receive what was promised, because God had provided something better for us, so that apart from us they would not be made perfect." We, because of the indwelling Holy Spirit, have clarity concerning the glory of the Lord that the Old Testament believer could not have. In those days it was a glory that was fading and had to be renewed by Moses' going and communing with the Lord. Beholding His glory became codified under the Old Covenant by the repetitive sacrifices. The writer of Hebrews captures this difference between Old Testament believers and New Testament believers this way:

> *For since the law has but a shadow of the good things to come instead of the true form of these realities, it can never, by the same sacrifices that are continually offered every year, make perfect those who draw near. Otherwise, would they not have ceased to be offered, since the worshipers, having once been cleansed, would no longer have any consciousness of sins?"*
> *(Heb. 10:1–2, ESV)*

But we have unveiled faces because of the New Covenant—because of Christ's one-time, single sacrifice. Again in Hebrews 10:14 (ESV), "For by a single offering he has perfected for all time those who are being sanctified." So our faces are unveiled and we are constantly able to reflect the glory of the Lord as we gaze upon that glory.

This transformation happens as we behold as in a mirror—as we reflect the Lord's glory. For you and me, what are some aspects of beholding the Lord's glory?

Look at the Son

The opening verses of the letter to the Hebrews tells us that God has spoken to us through His Son, who is the radiance of God's glory and the exact representation of His nature. If you want to see His glory, look at the Son. Behold His omnipotence in calming the sea, His compassion in weeping over Lazarus, His omniscience in knowing exactly what the Pharisees were thinking as in Luke 7,[38] His mercy toward the Syrophoenician woman of Matthew 15, and His righteousness in cleansing the temple as in John 2. Meditate on the life of Christ.

Read and Meditate on God's Word

> *"Your word is a lamp to my feet*
> *and a light to my path"*
> *(Ps. 119:105).*

There is glory in God's Word. When Moses went to the Sinai to receive the law from God, there was glory (see Exodus 33–34; 2 Corinthians 3). The prophet Isaiah in telling of the future millennium said:

> *A voice is calling,*
> *'Clear the way for the LORD in the wilderness;*
> *Make smooth in the desert a highway for our God.*
> *Let every valley be lifted up,*
> *And every mountain and hill be made low;*
> *And let the rough ground become a plain,*

---

38   The entire episode is in Luke 7:36–50 but specifically verses 39–40. Jesus obviously knew what the Pharisee Simon was thinking when He told him the parable of the two debtors.

> And the rugged terrain a broad valley;
> **Then the glory of the LORD will be revealed,**
> **And all flesh will see it together;**
> **For the mouth of the LORD has spoken.'**
> (Isa. 40:3–5)

When the Lord Jesus Christ was glorified on the mount of transfiguration, the Word of God was there when He said, "'This is My beloved Son, with whom I am well-pleased; listen to Him!'" (Matt. 17:5). On the mount of transfiguration, Peter, James, and John beheld God's glory in looking to the Son, but it was in the hearing of the Word of God that the glory was so intense that they fell on their faces. We must spend time in His precious Word.

Proclaim the Gospel

The Word of God is the conduit for His glory (Ps. 87:3; John 17:14, 17, 22). And it is through the Word of God that the gospel is given.

> And even if our gospel is veiled, it is veiled to those who are perishing, in whose case the god of this world has blinded the minds of the unbelieving so that they might not see the light of the gospel of the glory of Christ, who is the image of God. For we do not preach ourselves but Christ Jesus as Lord, and ourselves as your bond-servants for Jesus' sake. For God, who said, 'Light shall shine out of darkness,' is the One who has shone in our hearts to give the Light of the knowledge of the glory of God in the face of Christ.
> (2 Cor. 4:3–6)

We behold Christ's glory when we give the gospel. Have you ever been reviled for the name of Christ? There is glory there. 1 Peter 4:14 says, *"If you are reviled for the name of Christ, you are blessed, because the Spirit of glory and of God rests on you."*

Big Changes Some Day

My friend, Paul Hoelzley, PhD, former professor of music at British Columbia's Trinity Western University, spent much of his professional career as a board certified music therapist. Now retired in Victoria, British Columbia, Paul formerly practiced in the United States and Canada and traveled to Japan through a grant from the Japan Research Foundation and the Yamaha Corporation to work with autistic children there. In Paul's Canadian clinical practice, he had a young client who suffered from global dyspraxia, "a neurologically based disorder that impedes the processes involving motor-planning and motor movement actions, including those actions necessary for the production of speech."[39] The young client's name was Tyrone. In short, Tyrone is not able to speak and has many other motor skill challenges. It was discovered, however, by Tyrone's speech therapist that he has a brilliant mind and is able to use the computer. He began writing his thoughts down. Tyrone, a believer in the Lord Jesus Christ, began writing seriously when he was eleven years old. Here is a poem Tyrone wrote about what will happen to God's children when Jesus returns. It is called, "Big Changes Some Day":

> *God will make us perfect someday*
> *Happy, so happy, we'll be perfect someday*
> *The nearer to Heaven the triumph is sure*

---

39 Tyrone Brown, Big Changes Some Day (Victoria, BC, Canada: firstchoice-books.ca, 2009), p. 1.

Great thought this will happen
He's promised it's true
Hope is so blessed the heart longs to see
The change to be like Him and perfect someday

Few will be asking the saints in that day
What were your trials and cause of dismay
The song in that day will be gladness and joy
Our Lord to behold Him
His likeness to wear
Dress us in glory forever to share
To be like Him, with Him and perfect someday[40]

In early childhood, Tyrone was labeled by psychologists as moderately mentally challenged. They did not understand the brilliant mind trapped inside him. Because of Jesus Christ, today Tyrone is a child of God, growing in Christlikeness inside a broken body. But there are indeed big things coming someday. The broken body will be redeemed, and Tyrone will be able to praise God with the voice, the words, and the song that he never had on this old earth. But, more importantly, all of his concerns about what others thought of him will be gone. His lack of contentment and his desire for the things of this earth will end.

What I am saying is that this is the hope, the inheritance for each of us who have trusted in Christ alone for our present and for our future. All tears will be wiped away. I will no longer indulge in melancholia. My tendency to lash out at others will be gone. My physical eyesight will be perfect, as will my spiritual eyesight.

---

40   Ibid., p. 80.

THIRTEEN

Dwellings

A New Tent

During our first three years of marriage, Pat and I lived in one of the most beautiful, picturesque areas of North America. We lived in Calgary, Alberta, Canada and spent those summers working in Banff National Park in the Canadian Rockies. I had never camped growing up, but working in such a place, camping was almost required. Pat, however, had grown up camping so we began what was to become a lifelong hobby.

During those first few "poor" years, we borrowed or rented camping equipment, and when we moved to Texas, we set our sights on Big Bend National Park, borrowed a work colleague's tent, and, with our two little boys in tow, set out for Rio Grande Village in Big Bend. We were in awe! It was magnificent! On what we thought was to be our last full day there, the wind came up early in the morning. I mean it really came up! The nearby Boquillas Canyon acted as a wind tunnel and made it impossible to eat breakfast outside the tent. While we were in the tent, a particularly strong gust came up and snapped one of the aluminum tent poles. So we got out of the tent, gathered our kids, our equipment, and the disabled tent, and headed home. We headed home because our tent was broken and unusable. Even though we had had a great time camping, when we got back home, it felt warm, familiar, and inviting. We got to sleep in our own comfortable beds.

Someday, all of us who have trusted Jesus Christ will feel that comfort of being home. We will head home because our tent is broken and unusable. The apostle Paul, a tentmaker by trade, uses the language of our bodies as tents to express the great truths of 2 Corinthians 5:1–8:

> *For we know that if the earthly tent which is our house is torn down, we have a building from God, a house not made with hands, eternal in the heavens. For indeed in this house we groan, longing to be clothed with our dwelling from heaven, inasmuch as we, having put it on, will not be found naked. For indeed while we are in this tent, we groan, being burdened, because we do not want to be unclothed but to be clothed, so that what is mortal will be swallowed up by life. Now He who prepared us for this very purpose is God, who gave to us the Spirit as a pledge. Therefore, being always of good courage, and knowing that while we are at home in the body we are absent from the Lord—for we walk by faith, not by sight—we are of good courage, I say, and prefer rather to be absent from the body and to be at home with the Lord.*

Now, when we begin chapter 5, we have some context. To be truly faithful to this tent metaphor of which Paul speaks, and what it really means for me as I focus on the future and not the past, I need to go all the way back to the last verse of chapter 3 and look at more concepts and imagery of chapter 4.

"But we all, with unveiled face, beholding as in a mirror the glory of the Lord, are being transformed into the same image from glory to glory, just as from the Lord, the Spirit" (2 Cor. 3:18).

> *Therefore, since we have this ministry, as we received mercy, we do not lose heart, but we have renounced the things hidden because of shame, not walking in craftiness or adulterating the word of God, but by the manifestation of truth commending ourselves to every man's conscience in the sight of God. And even if our gospel is veiled, it is veiled to those who are perishing, in whose case the god of this world has blinded the minds of the unbelieving so that they might not see the light of the gospel of the glory of Christ, who is the image of God. For we do not preach ourselves but Christ Jesus as Lord, and ourselves as your bond-servants for Jesus' sake. For God, who said, 'Light shall shine out of darkness,' is the One who has shone in our hearts to give the Light of the knowledge of the glory of God in the face of Christ. But we have this treasure in earthen vessels, so that the surpassing greatness of the power will be of God and not from ourselves; we are afflicted in every way, but not crushed; perplexed, but not despairing; persecuted, but not forsaken; struck down, but not destroyed; always carrying about in the body the dying of Jesus, so that*

the life of Jesus also may be manifested in our body. For we who live are constantly being delivered over to death for Jesus' sake, so that the life of Jesus also may be manifested in our mortal flesh. So death works in us, but life in you. But having the same spirit of faith, according to what is written, 'I BELIEVED, THEREFORE I SPOKE,' we also believe, therefore we also speak, knowing that He who raised the Lord Jesus will raise us also with Jesus and will present us with you. For all things are for your sakes, so that the grace which is spreading to more and more people may cause the giving of thanks to abound to the glory of God. Therefore we do not lose heart, but though our outer man is decaying, yet our inner man is being renewed day by day. For momentary, light affliction is producing for us an eternal weight of glory far beyond all comparison, while we look not at the things which are seen, but at the things which are not seen; for the things which are seen are temporal, but the things which are not seen are eternal. (2 Cor. 4:1–18)

2 Corinthians 3:18 points to that wonderful day when my glorification will be complete. "But we all, with unveiled face, beholding as in a mirror the glory of the Lord, are being transformed into the same image from glory to glory, just as from the Lord, the Spirit."

"From glory to glory," means that, more and more, I am being transformed into the image of Christ. I might add, transformed into His glorified image. Oh, you wouldn't know it! Sometimes I stink. Sometimes I hobble around with a strained Achilles tendon. Sometimes I say unkind things to people, and sometimes I remain silent when I should speak the gospel. But by His grace, even in this tent, in this nakedness, I am growing from positional glory to realized glory.

Paul sets up a series of contrasts. These contrasts show that what is to come for the believer in Jesus Christ is far superior to what has been in the past. In 2 Corinthians 3, we have the contrast between the Old Covenant (the Mosaic law), set against the New Covenant, inaugurated by the blood of Christ and energized by the Holy Spirit. In 2 Corinthians 4, we have contrast between the transcendent gospel of the glory of Christ (verse 4) set against the pathetic earthen vessels, our frail and fallible bodies, in which this treasure is carried (verse. 7). Death in us so that there will be life in you (verse 12). Note this paragraph from 2 Corinthians 4:7–12:

> But we have this treasure in earthen vessels, so that the surpassing greatness of the power will be of God and not from ourselves; we are afflicted in every way, but not crushed; perplexed, but not despairing; persecuted, but not forsaken; struck down, but not destroyed; always carrying about in the body the dying of Jesus, so that the life of Jesus also may be manifested in our body. For we who live are constantly being delivered over to death for Jesus' sake, so that the life of Jesus also may be manifested in our mortal flesh. So death works in us, but life in you.

We are told in verse 17 that momentary affliction is working for us an eternal weight of glory. For all the glory of the New Covenant, the believer's life is not easy. This is especially true for those whose lives are intentional in ministering the New

Covenant. For all the glory of the gospel of Jesus Christ, the bearing of that treasure is only possible by the power of God (verse 7). Then Paul goes on to describe the storms of life that have beat on him as a minister of the gospel. He describes being afflicted but not crushed, perplexed but not in despair, persecuted but not forsaken, and struck down but not destroyed (verses 8–9). How does this all relate to me? This tent of mine, this earthen jar, is invincible while there is work for me to do for Him on earth.

I can't help thinking of Paul's first missionary journey, recorded in Acts 13 and 14, when he was stoned in Lystra, dragged out of the city, and left for dead (Acts 14:19). In spite of his condition, Dr. Luke[41] simply tells us that Paul got up and went back into Lystra! And not only that, after he and Barnabas had gone to Derbe, preached the gospel and made many disciples, they turned around and came back through Lystra! Those four sets of contrasts in 2 Corinthians 4:8–9 were certainly on display in Paul's life. Are they on display in mine? Do I dare to do great things for God in spite of apparent danger? Yes, I am an earthen vessel. Yes, I am a baggy old tent. But until my course of carrying this precious treasure is done, I am invincible! Thus, I gladly lay down my life for the cause of Christ! Affliction may come because death works in me so that life might work in others! But here is the great promise of 2 Corinthians 4:14: "Knowing that he who raised up the Lord Jesus shall raise up us also by Jesus and shall present *us* with you."[42] We who labor in the gospel will be raised from the dead, as will those

---

41　Luke, the physician, is the same person who wrote the Gospel of Luke. He also wrote Acts. John MacArthur, editor, MacArthur Study Bible (New King James Version) (Nashville, London, Vancouver, Melbourne: Word Bibles, 1997), p. 1630.

42　C.I. Scofield, editor, The New Scofield Reference Bible-Authorized King James Version (New York, NY: Oxford University Press, 1967), p. 1,255,

who trust Christ through our witness. And the affliction which may come cannot be compared to the sure coming glory!

So we come to the tent metaphor. Tent is the Greek word, σκῆνος —*skenos*.[43] It can be translated here as "tent" or "tabernacle." In any case, it refers to a temporary dwelling. Don't skim over that. It refers to a temporary dwelling. The occupant of such a temporary dwelling has no intention of living there permanently. Our culture is deluded into believing that this temporary dwelling is all there is. They are to be exercised, nourished, made love to, made up, facelifted, and when further improvement is impossible, removed from sight, burned up, and remembered with earlier photos when it was in its glory years. From the fall of man, that was never God's plan for these tents. The winds of the sin nature, the winds of this world wear down the tent, our bodies. Oh, we can be patched up with ibuprofen, surgery, exercise, and various injections, but eventually even these helps stop working. The tent wears down. It tears down. In fact, it is torn down. The Greek word that is used can mean "to abolish or overthrow."[44] Interestingly, in ancient Greek secular literature, it could be used to describe striking a military encampment, taking down the tents, and moving on. For us, our tents, our current bodies, will simply be cremated or buried in the ground. It has been said that there are no people buried in cemeteries. There are only worn-out bodies, worn-out tents.

The tent or tabernacle is for the purpose of temporarily housing the real person! And that real person, or at least the real person who has been clothed with the robe of Christ's

---

43   "2 Corinthians 5: King James Version (KJV)," Blue Letter Bible, https://www.blueletterbible.org/kjv/2co/5/1/t_conc_1083001, accessed February 21, 2022.

44   "Lexicon: Strong's G2647 – katalyō," Blue Letter Bible, https://www.blueletterbible.org/lexicon/g2647/kjv/tr/0-1/, accessed February 21, 2022.

righteousness, groans in that tent with the eager expectation, the sure hope of occupying our dwelling (οἰκητήριον —*oiketerion*) from heaven. This dwelling is our permanent residence, the resurrection body!

Groaning

While we wait, however, we groan. We sigh. Why? Because we so strongly desire this resurrection body. This heavenly dwelling. Sometimes, I suppose in a trivial sort of way, I remark about wanting a full head of hair and a mind that doesn't forget things or is good at math. But the Scripture is correct. The real reason I groan in this body is because I want what is mortal to be swallowed up by life. Reader, how often do you think about death? Your death? Throughout the whole of human history, the death rate has been nearly 100 percent. I look forward to my resurrection body on the new earth because I will never need to think of that again! I groan for that time!

Several months ago, I was visiting family in West Virginia. I particularly enjoyed the time I spent with my brother and his wife. My brother pastors a church in West Virginia, and, during the week that I was there, they were having a series of special meetings with a guest speaker. The guest speaker was Dr. Glenn Mathews, a gentleman in his mid-eighties, who has had a local radio ministry for many years. One evening, this godly man gave a message on his least favorite verse in the Bible. It is James 4:17: "Therefore, to one who knows *the* right thing to do and does not do it, to him it is sin." It was a message that encouraged many of us to greater obedience to God's Word and greater obedience to the promptings of the Holy Spirit. Then this preacher stopped and, with what I can only describe as a sigh or a groan, he said, "I am so tired of needing to confess my sins to God. I will be so happy when I am where there is no sin." I believe that this is the deepest sense in which the believer groans. What anticipation we have of being free from the very presence of sin! Several verses before our current passage, we read, "Now. . .where the Spirit of the Lord is, *there* is liberty" (2 Cor. 3:17). Do you groan for the ultimate escape from sin? What liberty!

This is different from the pressing on to maturity in this life that we saw in Philippians 3. This is longing, groaning for the mortal to put on immortality. This is longing for the resurrection body promised in both the Old Testament and New. In Philippians 3, Paul is concerned mostly with striving for the goal of Christlikeness in this life. In 2 Corinthians 5, he is concerned with the complete resurrected body on the new earth.

Pressing on to maturity in the Christian life like a runner in a race and groaning to be in the presence of the Lord in a new resurrection body, free from sin, are parallel tracks. Being on those tracks leads to the destination of eternity with Christ and in conformity with Christ. This is God's plan for the life of each of His children.

FOURTEEN

Contentment II

I am further along in the grieving process than I was when I wrote the previous chapter on contentment. I have become increasingly convinced that contentment is a major component in healing after the loss of any loved one, particularly after the loss of a spouse. I think this frame of mind deserves more treatment, so I want to look at some very hard but very practical instructions from 1 Corinthians 7.

1 Corinthians 7:7–8 tells me that my current state is a gift from God: "*Yet I wish that all men were even as I myself am. However, each man has his own gift from God, one in this manner, and another in that. But I say to the unmarried and to widows that it is good for them if they remain even as I.*"

Granted, the context is marriage and celibacy. And the apostle is stating that both are gifts from God. The very practical instruction here is this: The widow and the widower are sexually experienced people. We may look back with longing on that period of our lives. But God can and often does give the gift of celibacy to one to whom He had not previously given it.

I sometimes have the wicked thought to pray, "Father, this gift of celibacy that you want to bless me with? I don't want it!" What an offense to my Father, Provider, Savior, Redeemer, Comforter, Refuge, and Friend! What is this but an indication that the idolatry of self-indulgence that I thought was crucified in my life is still very much alive and kicking. Is not my heavenly Father's intimate communion with me better than the communion that I have with a wife, another sinner like me?

Elisabeth Elliot said this:

> *Single life may be only a stage of a life's journey, but even a stage is a gift. God may replace it with another gift, but the receiver accepts His gifts with thanksgiving. This gift for this day. The life of faith is lived one day at a time, and it has to be lived—not always looked forward to as though the 'real' living were around the next corner. It is today for which we are responsible. God still owns tomorrow.*[45]

Cultivating the Communion

Like the child raised in the church who knows all the right answers, I know the answer I am supposed to give to the question, "How do I cultivate communion with God?" But the actual doing of it depends on how badly I want communion with the Almighty. Shall I discipline myself to carve out time for undistracted prayer? Shall I read His Word in a deep and devoted way, and not as though I'm reading the newspaper? And what about the temptations that so easily come to a man who is living alone? How shall I fiercely treat them as the enemy of my soul and the barrier to intimacy with the Holy One that they are?

---

45 Elisabeth Elliot, "Let Me Be a Woman Quotes," goodreads, https://www.goodreads.com/work/quotes/121519-let-me-be-a-woman, accessed February 21, 2022.

Solomon wrote vividly, and erotically of marital intimacy. He wrote in this way in the Song of Solomon and also in Proverbs, particularly in chapter 5.

> *Drink water from your own cistern*
> *And fresh water from your own well.*
> *Should your springs be dispersed abroad,*
> *Streams of water in the streets?*
> *Let them be yours alone*
> *And not for strangers with you.*
> *Let your fountain be blessed,*
> *And rejoice in the wife of your youth.*
> *As a loving hind and a graceful doe,*
> *Let her breasts satisfy you at all times;*
> *Be exhilarated always with her love.*
> *(Prov. 5:15–19)*

But how do I make my celibate life ring with such ardor? Ardor of a different sort but still with a passion that satisfies the deepest longing of my soul? The answer is found in part in Psalm 37:4:

"*Delight yourself in the LORD; and He will give you the desires of your heart.*"

In other words, there is a certain intimacy with God suggested by this delight. As a husband and wife grow closer by sweet intimacy, their likes and dislikes grow together. They have shared dreams, shared desires. So by personal, intimate, spiritual time with God in worship of Him, His desires become my desires. I can bask in sweet communion with Him, allowing His desires to become my desires. Here is real contentment!

Jesus Is Enough

When Joy, the young woman I wrote of in chapter 9, said to me, "I've lost everything, but I have Jesus now," I wanted her to continue that sentence with one more phrase. I wanted her to say, "and Jesus is enough." But she didn't. She stopped abruptly as though that phrase was on the tip of her tongue, and she just couldn't say it. In times of profound grief, the things we believe, the things we know to be true, are challenged. I believe that at the moment she stopped talking, Joy wanted to say, "Jesus is enough," but happy images of her life with her husband and her daughter and fleeting thoughts of what might have been with the child she was carrying temporarily blotted out the truth that Jesus is enough. These images and thoughts are powerful emotional bombs. If not for the power of the indwelling Holy Spirit keeping the believer, these bombs could destroy the foundations of our faith.

For me, realizing my weaknesses makes some of the towering pronouncements of Job, who suffered more than most mortals ever will, quite astounding when he said:

> 'Naked I came from my mother's womb,
> And naked I shall return there.
> The LORD gave and the LORD has taken away.
> Blessed be the name of the LORD.'
> (Job 1:21)

> 'Though He slay me,
> I will hope in Him.'
> (Job 13:15)

> 'As for me, I know that my Redeemer lives,
> And at the last He will take His stand on the earth.

> *Even after my skin is destroyed,*
> *Yet from my flesh I shall see God.'*
> *(Job 19:25–26)*

I will not comment extensively on any of these pronounce-ments individually because I want to point out a common theme. It is indeed also the theme of this book. How does a person stop looking at the past with such clarity and start look-ing ahead by the clarity of faith?

> *'Naked I came from my mother's womb*
> *[looking back],*
> *And naked I shall return there [looking ahead].*
> *The LORD gave and the LORD has taken away*
> *[past and present].*
> *Blessed be the name of the LORD [future].'*
> *(Job 1:21)*

> *'Though He slay me [present],*
> *I will hope in Him [future].'*
> *(Job 13:15)*

> *'As for me, I know that my Redeemer lives [present],*
> *And at the last He will take His stand on*
> *the earth [future].*
> *Even after my skin is destroyed,*
> *Yet from my flesh I shall see God [future].'*
> *(Job 19:25–26)*

Even early in Job's suffering, He is looking ahead. In Job 1:21, his forward look seems hazy. In Job 13:15 there seems to be more certainty, more clarity about the future. And finally, in

Job 19:25–26, he has the most clarity of all about a coming Redeemer who will conquer death. There is even clarity about Job's own death and his coming resurrection. I think it is important to remember that even after chapter 19, Job has much more suffering and many more questions to come before there is resolution. If Job were living on this side of the cross, I believe we would hear him say in these three pronouncements, "Jesus is enough."

Habakkuk is one of my favorite Old Testament characters. He was the prophet whose confusion was turned to confession. His anguish melted into adoration.[46] Habakkuk's problem was not that he needed to stop focusing on the past to look at the future that God had for him. Indeed, he needed to look beyond God's pronouncement of judgment on Judah at the hand of the Babylonians to God's future blessing of Israel. Habakkuk was a realist. This makes his great faith statement all the more worshipful.

> *Though the fig tree should not blossom,*
> *nor fruit be on the vines,*
> *the produce of the olive fail*
> *and the fields yield no food,*
> *the flock be cut off from the fold*
> *and there be no herd in the stalls,*
> *yet I will rejoice in the LORD;*
> *I will take joy in the God of my salvation.*
> *GOD, the Lord, is my strength;*
> *he makes my feet like the deer's;*
> *he makes me tread on my high places.*
> *(Hab. 3:17–19, ESV)*

---

46   J. Ronald Blue (commentator for Habakkuk), The Bible Knowledge Commentary: Habakkuk (USA: Victor Books, 1985), p. 1,507.

Habakkuk is another Old Testament saint who would have said, despite barrenness and want, "Jesus is enough." In the agrarian society of Habakkuk's day, such a scenario would have meant that he had no material resources. Nothing. Yet, by faith, he would rejoice in the Lord. By faith he would affirm that the Lord was his strength.

If there was ever a person in the entire canon of Scripture who was without resources, it was the thief on the cross in Luke 23. Justly condemned to death, his execution was in progress.[47] Yet, as his life blood poured from his body, he was miraculously able to respond to the prompting of the Holy Spirit, and say, "'Jesus, remember me when You come in Your kingdom!'" (Luke 23:42). And the God-Man was able to respond, "'Truly I say to you, today you shall be with Me in Paradise'" (Luke 23:43). I believe his song as he entered paradise with Jesus was, "Jesus is enough." I believe that is his song to this very day!

So many times since July 2016, I have cried out to God and said, "I have no strength, Lord. Help!" To have said that I was weak would imply that there was a little bit of strength. But I recognized that I had no resources. No strength. So I have learned to say, "I have Jesus, and Jesus is enough." As that truth becomes more and more clear to me and more and more precious to me, my vision for my future is more exciting.

---

47   What about the other thief? Could he not at least have taken a tentative step of faith? But no, he elected to hurl abuse at Jesus (Luke 23:39). Early in my Christian life, this seemed incredible. He, too, was dying and was without hope. But he continued to reject Jesus. I have been at the bedside of men who had only a few days to live and yet rejected Jesus and His gospel. What a tragedy!

FIFTEEN

Many Lessons Learned

Melanoma

As I was writing this book, I was diagnosed with melanoma, the deadliest form of skin cancer. That diagnosis sent me to yet another place I have never been before with my heavenly Father. Intimate prayer. Worshipful prayer. Intensely seeking prayer and deeper understanding of His Word and His work in my life.

My dermatologist had moved to a new practice, from Austin to San Antonio, and her new practice did not have my medical records. I knew it must be nearly time for my yearly exam, so I had the records transferred to the new practice and set up the appointment.

"Hmm. Look behind his ear here. Slightly darker pigment. Irregular. It may or may not be 'something,' but with his family history, we should biopsy it." A few days later I got the word that it was indeed a superficial melanoma and that it was probably caught early enough to be treated without oncology.[48]

But the fact that this cancer, hidden behind my left ear, was caught at such an early stage, the fact that it was the same

---

48   The Mohs surgeon was indeed able to remove all the cancer without
further treatment needed.

cancer that killed my mother at the age of thirty-five, and that I got the diagnosis less than a year after Pat left, made me understand that God had a very special purpose for it. The purpose for that cancer diagnosis was to teach me to be much more intentional, much more all in, much more determined to carve out of my life that which is least helpful in furthering God's kingdom.

There is quite an impressive scar behind my ear. Really a crater. I was given the option of a skin graft or letting the surgical wound heal slowly and naturally. I chose the latter. The slow but sure healing of that wound parallels the grief process. For a number of weeks, it needed to be bandaged and cleaned daily. There was a kind of self-consciousness about this bandage on my ear when I went out in public. Likewise, when Pat was gone, I remained covered up for a long time. I do not mean that I became a recluse, nor that I tried to hide my grief. It was just that I was so raw that I was not able to function in any near normal way at all. I have been learning that self-isolation is common to most people going through the grief process. Only those closest to me truly understood my isolation. The daily cleansing with tears was most necessary. Two times during the healing process of my surgical wound, I accidentally tore the scab off the wound. It hurt and it bled. In this time of mourning, the grieving scab has torn off more than twice. It happened at the supermarket trip and while pressure washing the driveway. It happened when I heard a great hymn that Pat loved so much sung by a great choir. All of these things ripped the scab off my mourning. But as the physical scab gets smaller each time, so does the emotional scab of pain. I am told that my surgical wound may take up to a year to completely heal. And even when it does, there will be an unnatural hollow spot on the back of my ear. Likewise, I am sure that even when my grief is healed, as it will someday be, there will still be that hollow spot left by my Patty's absence. But just as this particular melanoma didn't kill me, but left a scar, Pat's homegoing will not destroy me, despite the impressive scar it leaves.

As I began writing this book on Christmas Day 2020, I had one desire: to turn my attention from mourning the loss of the most precious earthly possession I ever had—literally 2020 hindsight—to looking to the future with excitement and anticipation of what God is doing and will do with my life, first on this old earth and then for the endless, fathomless whole of all eternity.

And what better way could God do that for me but to give me a new lease on life in a very tangible way? Not that I am guaranteed another twenty to thirty years on this old earth, but, even if I am struck with lightning later today and am suddenly in His presence, it will be, to paraphrase Reepicheep, the talking mouse of Narnia, with my face to the sunrise.[49] It will be, in agreement with the great apostle Paul, in the midst of "press[ing] on toward the goal for the prize of the upward call of God in Christ Jesus" (Phil. 3:14).

His Plans Are Better Than My Ideas

When I first started thinking seriously of retirement from teaching at the university, I began making serious plans for my life after retirement. I was looking to the future with confidence. I was making my plans for Pat and me. Yes, I was even praying about those plans. We would be true empty nesters. There would be more time to spend together. There would be

---

49   It is the genius of C.S. Lewis that he could create a talking mouse by the name of Reepicheep and give him such utterance as to stir the reader to tears. C.S. Lewis, "The Voyage of the Dawn Treader," in The Chronicles of Narnia (New York, NY: HarperCollins, 1952), p. 213. There read Reepicheep's speech telling of his great desire to be with Aslan, the Christ-figure, forever.

more uninterrupted ministry opportunities for the two of us together. We would do more overseas mission trips and would spend more time with our growing number of grandchildren. These plans were simply ideas. Yes, ideas put before God in prayer but still ideas. Oh, it was going to be wonderful, globetrotting with the gospel, visiting our kids often and lots of street evangelism spreading the gospel. Maybe we could even buy a two-person kayak and fish the flats of the Texas Gulf Coast together. Such were our ideas.

But God had a plan. And it actually included some of the ideas we had, though through circumstances we never would have chosen. We did spend more time together, much of it driving to and from Austin to doctor appointments and chemo treatments. There were more evangelism opportunities, many of them with dying cancer patients in the "chemo room." There were even global mission trips—for me. Pat stayed home and prayed. We had time with our grandchildren. We got to watch the oldest three, Jaylee, Averie, and Braeden, profess their faith in the Lord Jesus Christ and be baptized. From the day Pat was diagnosed to the day she went home, we welcomed four new grandbabies into the world, Priscilla, Zoe, Lidia, and Gabriel. God's plan was better than our idea.

And so it is now as I look to the future. I still have my ideas even now. And God still has His plans even now, and His plans are better than my ideas, though some of my ideas might be included in His plans. Looking to the future, I am more aware of the frailty of life on this old earth. It is good and proper for the Christ-follower to formulate ideas for his life on this old earth, ideas by which he can glorify God and make an eternal difference in people's lives. Sanctified ideas are only sanctified if they are conceived apart from the fear of death. My scriptural assignment is to fear God, not to fear death.

The World Is Watching

Someone has said that the Christian mourner is a gazingstock to the world. Our grief is a unique opportunity to show the unbelieving world that God is worth worshiping. I'm not sure that "gazingstock" is the best way to describe us, for "gazingstock" can mean that we are looked at with curiosity or contempt. The only two times the word is used in the King James Bible (Nahum 3:6 and Heb. 10:33), it has the idea of contempt. So I will simply say that the world of Christians and non-Christians is watching us. We who mourn and also name the name of Christ have opportunities that we have never had before to make Christ look great, to magnify Him. How can we magnify Christ? We can express gratitude for God's grace amid the storm. We can express confidence that suffering is the prelude to glory for the believer. We can also express confidence that we will see our loved one again in the very presence of God if she/he died in Christ. We can turn to an unbeliever who is seeking to comfort us and tactfully give the gospel to him.

There Is a Wonderful Future That I Cannot See

When we come to the book of Ezra, we come near the chronological end of the Old Testament. Judah has been in captivity in Babylon/Persia for seventy years. Now, the Persian King Cyrus signs an edict allowing the Jews to return to their land and Zerubbabel is appointed governor of Judah. Almost immediately, Zerubbabel begins rebuilding the temple that had been destroyed by the Babylonians near the beginning of the captivity. The temple that had been destroyed was none other than Solomon's temple, that previously glorious edifice that had housed the very Shekinah glory of God (See 2 Chronicles 7).

So when Zerubbabel completed the foundation of this new temple, it made sense that he wanted it as much like the original temple as possible. Ezra 3:10–13 tells us this:

> *Now when the builders had laid the foundation of the temple of the LORD, the priests stood in their apparel with trumpets, and the Levites, the sons of Asaph, with cymbals, to praise the LORD according to the directions of King David of Israel. They sang, praising and giving thanks to the LORD, saying, 'For He is good, for His lovingkindness is upon Israel forever.' And all the people shouted with a great shout when they praised the LORD because the foundation of the house of the LORD was laid. Yet many of the priests and Levites and heads of fathers' households, the old men who had seen the first temple, wept with a loud voice when the foundation of this house was laid before their eyes, while many shouted aloud for joy, so that the people could not distinguish the sound of the shout of joy from the sound of the weeping of the people, for the people shouted with a loud shout, and the sound was heard far away.*

The old men were weeping, presumably because Solomon's temple was so much more magnificent. They were remembering what was, but now was not.

However, Haggai the prophet, a contemporary of Zerubbabel, corrected this thinking. I can hear Haggai saying, "Zerubbabel, you, Joshua the high priest, and all the people who are remembering the magnificence of Solomon's temple, you think this temple is nothing by comparison. Right? Right. But I want you to know that God says that He Himself is going to be right in the midst of this temple. He will fill it with glory." He told them a lot more (see Haggai 2:1–9). But the point is this: Five hundred years later, God Incarnate would walk into this temple and offer Himself as Israel's King, the fulfillment of the Davidic covenant (See Luke 19).

Here is the danger of looking wistfully back. We have no ability to see what God may be doing in the future. It took the prophet of God to reveal to these builders what God would do. The lesson for me is easy. Look ahead. Strain. Stand on tiptoes. Expect great things from God in the future!

Epilogue

Pat and I were quite different from one another in many ways. Very few of those differences required major adjustments for either of us. Many of the differences were complementary. Some never were resolved and led to little humorous jibes at each other. One of these was Pat's love of jigsaw puzzles and my aversion to them. Whenever there was a new puzzle in the house, pieces would be spread out on the dining room table and the box lid with the picture on it prominently in view. She and a couple of our kids would search and search for the right pieces to fit in just the right places until the puzzle matched the picture on the box.

For most of our marriage, I was putting together a life puzzle, using the picture that I thought was God's picture for our life together. Then on one summer day in 2016, it began to dawn on me that there was a different picture on a different box than the one I had been piecing together. I had to begin finding new pieces of different shapes and different colors than those I had been using. And when "until death do us part" came, I had to stand back and realize that this married family life puzzle I had been working on was only part of a larger mosaic. One that continues to this day. So I am frequently on my knees asking, "Is this the right picture, Lord? Are these the right pieces?"

Are there certain activities, perhaps even entire mir
I must cut out of my life in order to throw myself ir
ministries with more energy? This excising may br

it may be freeing. But God has a specific call on my life that He has gone to lengths to point out to this old dullard.

Mourning is the air we breathe on this old earth. Anyone who lives long enough will lose someone he loves and will mourn that loss. Many of the sounds of the fallen natural world are squeaks, squawks, howls, cries, and calls in a minor key. But I and all who are my spiritual descendants must occupy—literally "[d]o business" (Luke 19:13)—until the Lord Jesus Christ returns. The groans and suffering of childbirth will be over. The new heaven and the new earth will have been born. The fact that Jesus "abolished death and brought life and immortality to light through the gospel" (2 Tim. 1:10) will no longer be faith but bold-faced sight. Occupy until He comes (Luke 19:13).

Occupy by the Spirit's power. Though the world and its death march would knock the mourner back into despair, and though he be, as David described, surrounded with the cords of death (Ps. 18:4–5), occupy. In the name of Jesus the Messiah who won the victory over death and in whose righteousness we stand, occupy. Though there is no strength, no soundness of flesh, no innate integrity of character, occupy by the Spirit's power. In the name of the One who lives eternally in a literal resurrection body in the presence of His heavenly Father, face with hope the hopeless zeitgeist of this present time.

We, as Christ-followers, must brace ourselves for whatever comes in this old world. And the worst will come. Be it the death of a spouse, a child, a parent, or a friend. But even if the Christ-follower were to make it all the way through life without ever experiencing one of these, as unlikely as that is, the best is yet to come! I have frequently used the adjective "old" to describe the present earth on which we live. I do that intentionally to distinguish this current earth from the one that is coming. The new heaven and the new earth are coming.

On this new earth, there will be no sin and no evidence of the corrupting influence of sin. The apostle John says it this way in Revelation 21:1–4 (NLT):

> *Then I saw a new heaven and a new earth, for the old heaven and the old earth had disappeared. And the sea was also gone. And I saw the holy city, the new Jerusalem, coming down from God out of heaven like a bride beautifully dressed for her husband. I heard a loud shout from the throne, saying, 'Look, God's home is now among his people! He will live with them, and they will be his people. God himself will be with them. He will wipe every tear from their eyes, and there will be no more death or sorrow or crying or pain. All these things are gone forever.'*

My Final Answer

At the beginning of this book, I said that my goal was to learn how to redirect my focus to the future and not the past. So there are two things I must do to be successful at this. One of them is to invest my life in others, especially to invest my life in others who are in pain. I recently met a man whose twenty-one-year-old son, addicted to opioids, died after taking just one too many pills. The man wept uncontrollably as he told me. This man needs to know the hope that I know. He needs God's comfort that I have experienced. How can I not invest my life in this man?

The other one is to trust fully that no matter what the past has been and no matter what the future will be here on this old earth, the best truly is yet to come.

*Blessed be the God and Father of our
Lord Jesus Christ, the Father of mercies and God of
all comfort, who comforts us in all our affliction so that we will be able to comfort those who
are in any affliction with the comfort with
which we ourselves are comforted by God.*

(2 Cor. 1:3–4)

Bibliography

1. Bennett, Arthur, ed. *The Valley of Vision: A Collection of Puritan Prayers & Devotions*. Reprint, Edinburgh, England: Banner of Truth Trust, 2020.

2. Blue, J. Ronald (commentator for Habakkuk). *The Bible Knowledge Commentary: Habakkuk*. USA: Victor Books, 1985.

3. Brown, Tyrone. *Big Changes Some Day*. Victoria, BC, Canada: firstchoicebooks.ca, 2009.

4. Burroughs, Jeremiah. "Sermon I." Blue Letter Bible. https://www.blueletterbible.org/Comm/burroughs_jeremiah/the-rare-jewel/sermon-one.cfm, accessed June 10, 2021.

5. *Cars*. Directed by John Lasseter. Produced by Pixar Animation Studios. Emeryville, CA: 2006.

6. Challies, Tim. "For the Christian Who Is Afraid To Die." Challies. Updated January 17, 2021. https://www.challies.com/quotes/for-the-christian-who-is-afraid-to-die/.

7. Challies, Tim. "The Ministry of Sorrow." Challies. Updated May 17, 2021. https://www.challies.com/articles/the-ministry-of-sorrow/.

8. "2 Corinthians 5: King James Version (KJV)." Blue Letter Bible. https://www.blueletterbible.org/kjv/2co/5/1/t_conc_1083001, accessed February 21, 2022.

9. Croce, Jim. Produced by Terry Cashman in the album "You Don't Mess Around With Jim." ABC Records, March, 1972. Lyrics: https://www.lyrics.com/lyric/35313890/Jim+Croce/Time+in+a+Bottle. License permission available from https://www.songfacts.com/facts/jim-croce/time-in-a-bottle, accessed February 21, 2022.

10. Elliot, Elisabeth. "Elisabeth Elliot Quotes." goodreads. https://www.goodreads.com/quotes/255854-to-be-a-follower-of-the-crucified-means-sooner-or, accessed February 21, 2022.

11. Elliot, Elisabeth. "Let Me Be a Woman Quotes." goodreads. https://www.goodreads.com/work/quotes/121519-let-me-be-a-woman, accessed February 21, 2022.

12. Francis. "All she had to do to get out of jail was to say, 'I recant.'" Huguenot Heritage. https://huguenotheritage.com/she-resisted/, accessed February 21, 2022.

13. Havergall, Frances. *Hymns for the Living Church.* Carol Stream, IL: Hope Publishing Company, 1974.

14. "Hebrews 13: New American Standard Bible 1995 (NASB95)." Blue Letter Bible. https://www.blueletterbible.org/nasb95/heb/13/2/po/t_conc_1146002, accessed February 21, 2022.

15. "Hospitable." Merriam-Webster. https://www.merriam-webster.com/dictionary/hospitable, accessed February 21, 2022.

16. "How did the things Jesus said and did when He was alone get recorded in the Gospels?" Got Questions. https://www.gotquestions.org/Jesus-alone.html, accessed July 25, 2021.

17. Hutchcraft, Ron. *Hope When Your Heart is Breaking.* Eugene, OR: Harvest House, 2021.

18. Lewis, C.S. "The Voyage of the Dawn Treader." Chap. 14 in *The Chronicles of Narnia.* New York, NY: HarperCollins, 1952.

19. "Lexicon: Strong's G2638 – *katalambanō.*" Blue Letter Bible." https://www.blueletterbible.org/nasb95/phl/3/12/p0/t_conc_1106012, accessed February 21, 2022.

20. "Lexicon: Strong's G2647 – *katalyō.*" Blue Letter Bible. https://www.blueletterbible.org/lexicon/g2647/kjv/tr/0-1/, accessed February 21, 2022.

21. "Lexicon: Strong's G447." Blue Letter Bible. https://www.blueletterbible.org/lexicon/g447/nasb95/mgnt/0-1/, accessed February 21, 2022.

22. "Lexicon: Strong's H7200." Blue Letter Bible. https://www.blueletterbible.org/lexicon/h7200/nasb95/wlc/0-1/, accessed August 3, 2021.

23. "Lexicon: Strong's H7503." Blue Letter Bible. https://www.blueletterbible.org/lexicon/h7503/nasb95/wlc/0-1/, accessed February 21, 2022.

24. Lincoln, Abraham. "Lincoln's First Inaugural Address." American Battlefield Trust. https://www.battlefields.org/learn/primary-sources/lincolns-first-inaugural-address, accessed February 21, 2022.

25. Lindsey, Hal and Carole C. Carlson. *The Late Great Planet Earth*. Zondervan Academic, 1970.

26. Lusko, Levi. *Through the Eyes of a Lion: Facing Impossible Pain, Finding Incredible Power*. Nashville, TN: W Publishing Group/Thomas Nelson, 2015.

27. MacArthur, John, ed. *MacArthur Study Bible* (New King James Version). Nashville, London, Vancouver, Melbourne: Word Bibles, 1997.

28. Matheson, George. *Hymns for the Living Church*. Carol Stream, IL: Hope Publishing Company, 1974.

29. Piper, John. *Don't Waste Your Cancer*. Wheaton, IL: Crossway Books, 2011. https://document.desiringgod.org/don-t-waste-your-cancer-en.pdf?ts=1439242114, accessed February 21, 2022.

30. Piper, John. *Don't Waste Your Life*. Wheaton, IL: Crossway Books, 2007.

31. Piper, John. *Future Grace*. Sisters, OR: Multnoma Publishers, 1995.

32. Piper, John. "Is It Sinful to Want to Die?" Desiring God, updated May 13, 2019, https://www.desiringgod.org/interviews/is-it-sinful-to-want-to-die.

33. Piper, John. *The Purifying Power of Living by Faith in Future Grace*. Sisters, OR: Multomah Publishers, 1995.

34. Scofield, C.I., ed. *The New Scofield Reference Bible-Authorized King James Version*. New York, NY: Oxford University Press, 1967.

35. Stanford, Miles J. *The Complete Green Letters*. Grand Rapids, MI: Zondervan, 1975, 1976, 1977, 1983.

36. Stifler, James A. *The Epistle to the Romans.* Thirteenth printing, Chicago, IL: The Moody Bible Institute of Chicago, 1979.

37. Tozer, A.W. *The Knowledge of the Holy.* New York, NY: HarperCollins, 1961.

38. Unger, Merrill F. *Unger's Bible Dictionary.* Chicago, IL: Moody Press, twenty-fourth printing, 1976.

39. Von Schlegel, Katharina A. *Hymns for the Living Church.* Carol Stream, IL: Hope Publishing Company, 1974.

EQUIPPEDMAMA
LLANO, TEXAS

Made in the USA
Monee, IL
02 June 2022